# THE LOST WORLD
## OF ELAM

# THE LOST WORLD OF ELAM

## OF ELAM

Re-creation of a Vanished
Civilization

Walther Hinz

Translated by Jennifer Barnes

SIDGWICK & JACKSON
LONDON

*This translation first published in 1972 in*
*Great Britain by Sidgwick and Jackson Limited*
*Originally published in West Germany*
*by Verlag W. Kohlhammer GmbH in 1964*
*Copyright © 1972 by Sidgwick and Jackson Limited*

*Translator's Note*

I should like to thank my brother, Nicholas Postgate, who originally proposed
this translation, who gave me much expert advice and saved me from
many mistakes; and my husband Jonathan, who patiently read the whole
translation, suggested many felicities, detected many errors, and encouraged
me from first to last.

J.M.B.

ISBN 0 283 97863 5

*Printed in Great Britain by*
*The Garden City Press Limited*
*Letchworth, Hertfordshire SG6 1JS*
*for Sidgwick and Jackson Limited*
*1 Tavistock Chambers, Bloomsbury Way*
*London WC1A 2SG*

# Contents

# List of Plates

# Preface

Until now the only practicable history of Elam has been George G. Cameron's *History of Early Iran*, published in Chicago in 1936, but this book is confined to Elam's political history. It is now supplemented by contributions from René Labat and from the author of the new edition of the *Cambridge Ancient History*. Yet these contributions do not cover the period after 1000 B.C., and an up-to-date publication giving an overall picture of Elam's history and civilisation is sadly missing.

This book is an attempt to supply, for the first time, a missing piece in the jigsaw of history which is 'Elam'. I have not only outlined external events, but have also described what we today can grasp of Elam's civilization: its language and script, its religion and law, and its art. Naturally, much remains uncertain due to inadequate sources and to their considerable linguistic difficulty.

For the dates of Mesopotamian history I have drawn mainly on the *Cambridge Ancient History*; those of Elam are largely the result of my own labours. They are based on the so-called 'middle chronology'. Hittite evidence, however, seems to favour the 'short chronology', in which case all the dates given for the third and second millennia B.C. ought to be reduced by sixty-two years in each case. I am deeply grateful to R. Borger, my Assyriological colleague in Göttingen, for his extensive advice on the cuneiform script. I should also like to thank the directors of the Louvre in Paris for permission to publish the photographs of Elamite monuments.

Göttingen

# Acknowledgements

Plates 4 and 19–32 were most kindly provided by Professor Dr André Parrot, Keeper of the Louvre, and were prepared by Maurice Chuzeville, of Paris.

Plates 9 and 10 (aerial views) were taken from the *Illustrated London News* of 13 July 1957 (pp. 76 and 77); Plate 9 is the work of Worldwide Surveys, Inc.; Plate 10 of M. Bahmani.

Plates 1–3, 5–8 and 11–18 are the author's.

Figures 1–17, 19–23, 25–28, 30–31, 33, 35–38 were drawn by Frau Gudrun Ulbrich of Göttingen from the texts listed below. Drawings 18 and 29 are the author's. Figures 24, 32, 34 and 39–42 have been reproduced exactly from the original publications.

# *Introduction*

Any educated man today knows of Sumer and Babylon, and has heard of the Hittites and Assyrians, of the Medes and Persians. But Elam has remained almost unknown. And yet, among the peoples of the ancient Near East, the Elamites enjoyed an outstanding culture and a history spanning more than two thousand years. Elam – today south-west Iran – is chary of investigation; as the French scholar M.-J. Steve wrote recently, after deciphering thousands of Elamite seal inscriptions, 'It is only with the greatest reluctance that Elam will consent to reveal her secrets.'* Last but by no means least, the Elamite language, which is one of the most intricate known to scholarship, obstinately resists elucidation.

It is to the Bible that Western civilization owes the preservation of at least the name of Elam. We find about a dozen occurrences of the name in the Old Testament, and even one in the New Testament. In the Acts of the Apostles (II :9) it is reported that among the Jews who were present at the events in Jerusalem at Pentecost were some from Elam. In Genesis (10 :22) Elam appears, it is true, as 'child of Sem'; but this has only a geographical connotation, in as much as the Elamites living on the plain bordering Mesopotamia were governed for a considerable period by Semites and even to some extent

* *Iranica Antiqua 2*, Leiden, 1962, 22

colonized by them. At another point in the same book (Genesis 14 : 1), a certain King Kedor-laomer, King of Elam, is mentioned. The name sounds authentic – in Elamite, Kuter-Lagamar would mean 'the [goddess] Lagamar is a protectress' – but is not as yet attested in inscriptions.

There is also a mention in the Book of Daniel (8 : 2) that is worthy of comment. In the third year of the regency of the Babylonian crown prince, Belshazzar, in 543 B.C., the prophet Daniel saw another vision 'at Shushan in the palace, which is in the province of Elam', and the archangel Gabriel interpreted the vision to him 'between the banks of the Ulai'.* During the two and a half thousand years since then, the once mighty capital of Susa on the Ulai has become the humble village of Shush on the Sha'ur. But the tomb, by tradition Daniel's grave, is sacred to Moslems and forbidden to Christians, and its curious honeycomb spire still dominates the village (Plate I).

The eastern side of Shush huddles beneath huge mounds many hundred metres long and in places over forty metres high. This mountain of deposit is all that now remains of a once considerable city. Where once stood the temple acropolis of Susa, there has towered since 1897 a building, battlemented like a fortress : the excavation headquarters of the French Archaeological Mission (Plate 2). At the time, this fortress amply justified its erection. The territory was unsafe and the inhabitants scarcely hospitable to the 'Franks' (Europeans). In 1850 the Englishman W. K. Loftus became the first man to suffer physically as a result of their attitude; he was forced to beat a hasty retreat while carrying out a survey of the ruined area. From 1884–6 Marcel Dieulafoy and his very able wife Jane, both French, braved the inhabitants to excavate in Susa. They were followed in 1889 by their compatriot Jacques de Morgan. Since the Paris government obtained a monopoly of excavation from the Shah, French archaeologists have been almost continuously active in Susa : de Morgan until 1913, then

---

* See my book *Zarathustra*, Stuttgart, 1961, p. 44, for details of Daniel's account, which reveals an exact knowledge of the geography of Susa.

Roland de Mecquenem, after 1936 Roman Ghirshman, and since 1969 Jean Perrot. It is to them that scholars owe the great majority of available monuments and inscriptions which we now possess on the history of Elam. The trial excavation undertaken by J. E. Gautier and G. Lampré over two months in 1903, in the area of *Tepeh Mussian*, roughly 150 kilometres north-west of Susa, resulted in no written evidence whatever.

In the year 1876, an 'epigraphical and archaeological expedition', sent under the auspices of the Prussian Ministry of Culture, was working in the far south of Elam, at what is now *Bushire* in the Persian Gulf, about four hundred kilometres from Susa; among them were Franz Stolze, the photographer, and F. C. Andreas, afterwards Professor of Iranian studies at Göttingen. On the southern half of the Bushire peninsula they discovered a barrow, containing hundreds of inscribed bricks dating from Elam's 'classical period' – that is, from the thirteenth to the twelfth centuries B.C. However, the bricks had to be abandoned when the expedition was unexpectedly recalled; 'and as no money was available for storage [here I quote Georg Hüsing] they were subsequently sold as souvenirs and became scattered around the globe; among their destinations were the museums of Paris, Leiden, the Hague and London. Dr Stolze was only able to bring two specimens to Berlin.' Then, in 1913, Maurice Pézard excavated the site now known as Sabzabad; in addition to the six inscriptions which the two Germans had salvaged from more than a thousand bricks buried in the clay, he recovered only two more.

The Elamites used to amuse themselves by inscribing the same word over and over again on clay tablets, which they then baked and put up as a decorative frieze on the temple walls. This habit is borne out *ad nauseam* by another Elamite site, *Choga Zambil*. This town, whose name means 'basket-hill' in the Lur Dialect, lies about forty kilometres south-south-east of Susa, not far from the righthand bank of the Diz. In about 1250 B.C., King Untash-napirisha founded a sacred city there (Dur-Untash or Al-Untash); at its heart there rose a vast stage-tower (in Babylonian, a ziggurat). In 1935, Brown, an oil prospector from New Zealand, had been intrigued while flying over the area to notice an enormous mound surrounded by two walls. Between 1951 and 1962, following preliminary excavations that had taken place before the First World War, the French Mission under Ghirshman's direction exposed the site which had until then lain hidden in the hill.

Among more than five thousand inscribed bricks which thus came to light, almost seventy per cent bore the same text ... it is easy to sympathize with the groans of Père Steve, who complained that the deciphering of a vow recurring on thousands of bricks led to eventual exhaustion. However, now that the excavations have been discontinued, Choga Zambil has reverted to its original isolation; jackals prowl through the ruins in broad daylight, and the only human being in sight is a Persian policeman. It is his duty to watch the ziggurat—and of course he cannot be held responsible if one brick after another vanishes mysteriously from the walls.

In 1962–3, the Oriental Institute at Chicago University, working through Pinhas Delougaz and Helene J. Kantor, undertook for the first time a dig on Elamite territory, at *Choga Mish* ('sheep-hill'), thirty kilometres east of Susa. They were only hoping for prehistoric finds. The same is true of the trial excavation completed by Frank Hole and Kent V. Flannery in 1961 at Ali Kosh, west of Mussian (to which I have already referred). It proved that this area had been colonized since the eighth millennium B.C.*

Otherwise, no excavations have been carried out in Elam to date. Sites of historical interest abound; a particularly promising one was rediscovered in 1962 by Dr F. G. L. Gremliza, a doctor from Swabia who had been living in the area for years. On one of his expeditions, he crossed the Diz on a ferry and eventually arrived at an extensive mound – a *tell* (in Arabic) or *tepeh* (in Persian) – from which an early settlement could be

---

* Since 1966, E. O. Negahban from the university of Teheran has been excavating the Elamite site near Haft Tepeh, between Ahwaz and Susa.

deduced (Plate 3). Wind and weather have so eroded the slope that Elamite tablets have emerged in several places. Dr Gremliza hastened to inform Ghirshman and Steve, the archaeologists at Susa. Fate smiled on them; their search in the soil was rewarded by the discovery of inscribed bricks of King Shutruk-nahhunte, from the early twelfth century B.C., and also of sherds dating back as far as 3000 B.C. Today, the place is known as *Deh-e nou* ('new village'); it lies about forty kilometres south-east of Susa, not on the right bank of the Diz like Choga Zambil, but on the further left bank; to be more precise, on a tributary called the Loreh. The area is no longer inhabited. When I went there on 4 March 1963, a black-and-yellow snake was sunning itself among the remains of Islamic buildings, and an owl gazed at me from a hole in the wall. Working from the inscribed bricks, Père Steve has been able to identify Deh-e nou with the important Elamite town of Hupshen, and to prove the existence of a temple to the goddess Manzat. The site would certainly repay further excavation.

To this testimony of Elamite civilization, revealed by excavation, must be added those plainly visible monuments preserved here and there. They include a large number of rock-carvings in the Bakhtiyar mountains, particularly around Izeh (once Malamir) and at Fahlian. The first European to venture into these remote parts was the Englishman A. H. Layard; his possessions were constantly plundered in the course of his dangerous expeditions between 1840 and 1842. He discovered countless memorial rock-carvings, many of which were not photographed till 1962 by the Belgian scholar L. Vanden Berghe (from Ghent). The most significant old Elamite rock-carving, brought to light in 1924 by Ernst Herzfeld of Berlin, is that at Kurangun (Plate 5), on the ancient military road from Susa to Persepolis, along which Alexander the Great penetrated the very heart of southern Iran in 330 B.C. Yet another relief, dating probably from the middle Elamite period, was discovered by chance in 1936, when Sir Aurel Stein happened to be in

Qal'e-ye Toll, south of Izeh. It was then forgotten until I un-covered it once more on 5 March 1963 (Plate 17). After being photographed, it was carefully returned to the soil, where it remains until it can be transferred to a museum.

As far as the publication of Elamite inscriptions is concerned, it is to Père Vincent Scheil that honour is primarily due. For decades he has toiled unremittingly to set out the results of the French excavations in his long series of *Mémoires*. After his death in 1940, the Dominican priest M.-J. Steve became epigraphist to the mission in Susa and he has now been replaced by François Vallat. From the first, the texts published by the French were eagerly studied both in Germany and in Austria.

In the thorny field of Elamite studies, certain men deserve special mention: F. H. Weissbach (killed in 1944 during a bombing raid on Leipzig); Ferdinand Bork (exiled from Königsberg, he died in Paderborn at an advanced age in 1962); Georg Hüsing, who died in Vienna in 1930; and Friedrich Wilhelm König, who died in 1972, also in Vienna. It is un-fortunate that the achievements of Hüsing and Bork are often marred by persistent prejudice and inaccuracy in their work. Beside Père Steve, whom I have already mentioned, the following scholars are now engaged on research into Elam: George G. Cameron (Ann Arbor, Michigan), René Labat and Pierre Amiet (Paris), Erica Reiner and Richard T. Hallock (Chicago), Piero Meriggi (Pavia), Yu. B. Yusifov (Babu), and the author. From time to time work on Elam has also been done by Johannes Friedrich (Berlin), Herbert H. Paper (Ann Arbor), and Maggie Rutten and Maurice Lambert (both at Paris). There are thus just a dozen Elamists in the world.

The deciphering of the Elamite script – of the linear script of ancient Elam and of the cuneiform that originated in Mesopotamia – will be dealt with in Chapter II.

# CHAPTER I

# Man in Ancient Elam

It is claimed by the Greek geographer Strabo (XV. 3. 10) that any snake or lizard that dared to crawl across the streets of Susa during the noonday heat of summer was roasted alive by the pitiless Elamite sun; and it is indeed a fact that M. Dieulafoy recorded 72°C. in the sun there one July midday, and Dr Gremliza 50° in the shade at the same time of year near Dizful. The mean temperature of Susiana in July is 38°C. The lowest winter temperature is about 5°, but by April summer heat prevails once more. In the period from 28 July to 8 August there begins a series of intolerable heatwaves, which only abate very gradually in September. So it is perhaps hardly surprising that the inhabitants of Shushtar and Dizful still spend their summer, whenever possible, underground, in cellars.

The plain of Elam, which has been known since the Middle Ages as Khuzistan by the Iranians, is roughly 42,000 square kilometres in area; this makes it about the size of Denmark. Geologically speaking, Susiana consists of a deposit of fine silt. It rises gradually towards the north from sea-level in the Persian Gulf to an average height of 100 metres around the present-day capital of Ahwaz. At the foot of the plateau of Luristan (now known as Andimeshk) it rises to a height of 170 metres.

Originally, the plain of Elam was a veritable storehouse of fruit and grain. The Sassanid kings (A.D. 224–638) improved the irrigation arrangements by employing Roman prisoners-of-war to build dams. Indeed, Susiana continued to thrive into the Middle Ages; Arabian geographers of the tenth century comment favourably on its sugar-cane harvest. But thereafter, the country began to degenerate. Large areas were ruined by salt because they lacked proper drainage. It was only with the coming of the oil industry that the province revived. For a long time, ever since 1908, the petroleum wells on the eastern side of Khuzistan have been tapped; but now drilling has proved successful even in the lowlands, near Ahwaz. And since 1961, after an interval of five hundred years, sugar-cane has once again been cultivated. A canal has also been constructed to irrigate the expanding plantations around *Haft Tepeh* (between Ahwaz and Susa); by local tradition it is known as the 'Darius Canal', but Ghirshman has shown that in fact it dates back to the Elamite King Untash-napirisha (*c.* 1250 B.C.). Early in 1963, Shah Mohammed Reza Pahlavi inaugurated a huge dam not far from Dizful; it was to transform Khuzistan from a grey-brown wilderness into a verdant and productive land. This dam, two hundred and three metres high, provides water for about 200,000 hectares of arable plain, and also provides the country with electricity; its annual output is 520,000 kilowatts. Khuzistan is thus in the throes of comprehensive change, rendering it in some ways comparable with the Susiana of Elamite times.

The plain owed its original fertility to its abundance of water-courses. No fewer than three rivers flowed through Susiana (Figure 1). Today, the most westerly is called the *Karkheh*; the Assyrians knew it as the *Uqnû* (lapis lazuli), the Greeks as the *Choaspes*. The Karkheh is as long as the Oder, and its water was famous for its purity and sweetness. The Greek 'father of history', Herodotus, informs us (I. 188) that Cyrus the Great (559–30) never went into battle without silver ewers of water from the Karkheh for his table, drawn by mules on four-wheeled carts. The middle river of Khuzistan is known today as the *Diz*; the Elamites and the Assyrians called

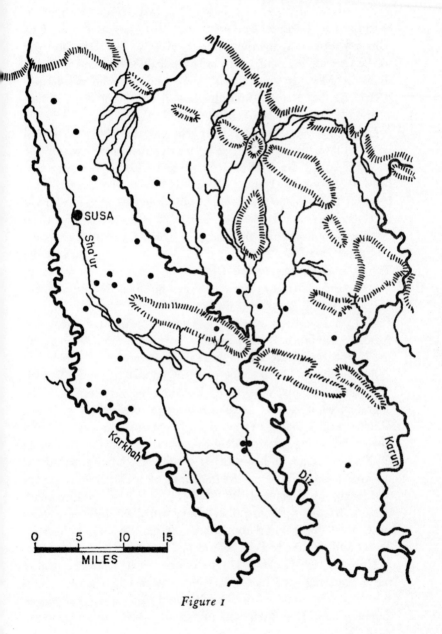

*Figure I*

it the *Idide,* and the Greeks the *Koprates.* The Diz rises at Borudjerd in Luristan, and joins the third river at Band-e-Qir. This is the *Karun,* the most easterly river in Susiana, *Pasitigris* to the Greeks; it is still Iran's only navigable river and is longer than the Elbe. It joins the Shatt-al Arab at Khorramshahr – where the Tigris and Euphrates become common water – and eventually flows into the Persian Gulf.

Originally, however, the Karkheh and the Diz were linked by a tributary of the Karkheh, partly man-made, which the Elamites called the *Ulai* and the Greeks *Eulaios.* But we know from the book of Daniel (8 : 16) that Susa, the capital, lay between two arms of the Ulai; it was therefore at the centre of an elaborate network of water-courses. It had access to the open sea along the Ulai and the Karkheh, which at that time flowed into the Persian Gulf (today it peters out in the marshes by the Tigris), and also along the Diz and the Karun. Nowadays, of course, the Ulai has become the humble Sha'ur, which, although it still flows into the Diz, westward past the tomb of Daniel, has lost its original connection with the Karkheh. Modern Iranian irrigation experts, however, would like to link the Karkheh and the Diz once again, this time by a canal.

Susa was also the meeting-point of important roads. Travelling westwards, you crossed the Karkheh by ferry, reaching the Tigris at what is now Amara in Iraq by three days' caravan; another week's journey would bring you to Babylon. A road had always led to the north, along the Karkheh and the Kashghan to Khurramabad in Luristan; it continued through Borudjerd towards modern Teheran, in the south of which is Rey, originally Raga, the Rhagai of the Bible (Tobias 1 : 14). A third road, passing through Shushtar, linked Susa with Izeh and the plateau of Isfahan; continuing southwards, it led through Behbehan, Basht, and Fahlian to Persepolis or to Shiraz.

However, in spite of its agricultural wealth, Susiana would never have regained its original importance had not the mountains of the north, east and south-east – namely modern Luristan and the Bakhtiyar mountains – been part of Elam.

The ancient Elamites called this mountainous area *Anzan* or *Anshan*, in particular the eastern part; both the town of Susa and the plain of Susiana bore the name of *Shushun*. The Sumerians used the logogram N I M for Elam; this means 'up' in their language. We may deduce from this that for the Mesopotamians, the true Elam lay 'up', not in Susiana but in the mountains behind. The Elamites themselves wrote the name of their country in cuneiform characters as *hal-ta-am-ti*, which could represent *Hal-tampt*; here *hal* would stand for 'land' and *tampt* for '[noble] lord'. This would imply that the Elamites saw their country as the 'land of the lord', or as the 'land of God'; this is, however, not certain.

The linking of the valley and the plateau (of Shushun and Anshan) was to prove decisive in the development of Elam's history and art, and herein lay its advantage over the neighbouring plains of Mesopotamia. The latter turned to the plateau of Elam for the raw materials of its cultural development. Thence, by trade or war, Sumerians or Babylonians imported their timber, their metals (copper, lead, tin and silver), their stone (basalt, marble, diorite, alabaster, arragonite and obsidian), their semi-precious stones (cornelian, bloodstone and lapis lazuli) and, not least, their horses.

Any attempt to trace the Elamites ethnologically is beset with difficulties. The more you investigate available sources, the more you get the impression that the Elamites were – the Elamites, a race of immutable independence. No relationship with other peoples has yet emerged. However, it seems likely that the Elamites had much in common with the Lullubi, a mountain race and their neighbours to the north, and with others of the so-called *Su* peoples. The Elamite population was nonetheless heterogeneous. In the glazed brick reliefs of his bodyguards with which Darius, King of the Persians, decorated the palace at Susa in 500 B.C., the artist clearly depicts three different races. Some guards are white skinned and are obviously intended to represent Persians, although in Elamite garb. A second group is brown-skinned and a third is very dark, almost black.

These must be Elamites from the hinterland. Even today dark-skinned men, in no way negroid, are often to be seen in Khuzistan. They consider themselves for the most part as Arabs, and speak Arabic among themselves. It seems likely that the population even of Ancient Elam was a mixed one, consisting of dark-skinned aboriginals of uncertain race and of Semites, who had infiltrated from Mesopotamia in repeated incursions since the Akkad period (twenty-fifth century B.C.).

The brown-skinned guards, on the other hand, may have represented the mountain Elamites, who survive today as the Lurs: in north Susiana the Feili-Lurs, in the east and south the Bakhtiyarians. The majority of the Lurs are black-haired and brown-skinned, a tough race, used to life in the mountains, and somewhat taller than the plain-dwellers. They too reveal an admixture of foreign blood, and thus cease to be pure 'Elamites'. But the admixture is less pronounced than in the valley Elamites, and its origin lies not in the Semitic but in the Indo-Germanic races, especially the Persians.

The end result of the Persian infiltration is that the Elamite Lurs have adopted only Persian speech since the Middle Ages. However, as late as A.D. 1000, Arab geographers still encountered an incomprehensible language here and there in Khuzistan. This *Khuzi* was clearly the last remaining variant of the Elamite language. The name *Khuzian* dates right back to ancient Persian times: even Darius the Great (522–486) knew of no Elam but only of a *Huzha*. The Huzhians were clearly the same as that Elamite race who, as Uxians, were reluctant to entrust themselves to Alexander's Greeks. The mountain Uxians were settled between Behbehan and Persepolis, a position dominating the road from Susa to Persepolis. When, as was their custom, they demanded toll from the passing Macedonian host, Alexander refused; however, he managed, not without difficulty, to force his way through their territory.

Information on the everyday life of the ancient Elamites is to be found in seals from the third millennium – information, it is true, by no means complete, but nonetheless revealing. The Elamite engravers have left us evidence of their surroundings and of the inhabitants, engaged on multifarious activities.

In these seal-impressions, the landscape of Susiana is depicted by winding rivers, where fish swim between rushy banks. Up on the plateau among pines, cedars, and terebinths, buffalo, chamois and mountain goats can be seen moving about. All kinds of animal inhabit the open ground or the undergrowth, graze peacefully or flee from lions. Then the Elamite hunter appears on the scene (Figures 2 and ). He is quite naked, or

*Figure 2*

*Figure 3*

clad only in a loin-cloth, and his weapons are bow and arrow, spear or pike. Accompanied by his dogs, he hunts the red deer, the antelope, the wild-boar or even the wild-cat. While in one place (Figure 4) naked fishermen drag giant tortoises to land, in another (Figure 5) an Elamite poles his boat, with its gracefully curved prow, to the bank. The captain of the boat, who has already disembarked, is carrying the prize fish, two large barbel, while his assistant follows him bearing a basket of smaller fish on his head.

Not far from the town, cattle are grazing; milk jars stand ready near the cows (Figure 6). Shepherds drive goats back to their crude brick stall; the entrance is flanked by a huge tower, and so the stall will probably belong to a palace or a temple (Figure 7). Whole armies of men are at work in the fields; they are preparing them for the sowing, using three-pronged hoes. This last seal-design (Figure 8) dates back four thousand years B.C., and its evidence is being confirmed by archaeological discoveries: Robert M. Adams of Chicago has recorded widely distributed stone axes, sickles of very hard-baked clay, and flint blades, all dating from Susiana of this period. This would indicate that axes and sickles were the main tools of the earliest Elamite peasants; but by about 3000 B.C., the plough appears on the seals (Figure 9). Women also help with the farming; we see them, clothed in wide smocks, working on the date-palm plantation (Figure 10).

In the town, all is bustle and activity. In the pottery workshop, stone vessels are being produced; while one man polishes the handle of a jar, other craftsmen smooth plates by rubbing them together (Figure 11). Women are also to be found in the workshops: they are seated on low wooden stools or on level ground, and are mostly occupied in preparing wool (Figure 12).

The granaries are particularly busy. According to the seals, the silos are constructed of mud bricks and are surmounted by a long series of domes. The exterior is provided with niches; between them and the flat roof stretches a row of narrow ventilation holes. Workers come and go with sacks or jars, bearing their burdens on head or shoulder, reaching the domes by ladder or by steps built on at the side (Figure 13). A terraced foundation raised the granaries above ground level; but there were also silos that were built partly underground, as is attested by a mathematical text found at Susa. Scribes squat near the granaries to record on their clay tablets each bushel of corn as it is delivered (Figure 14). Wine-stewards adopt the same position to fill their measures or to cork their jars (Figure 15).

What sort of people can these Elamites have been? The

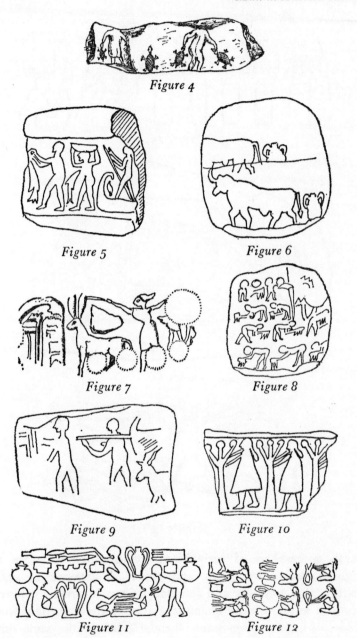

Figure 4

Figure 5

Figure 6

Figure 7

Figure 8

Figure 9

Figure 10

Figure 11

Figure 12

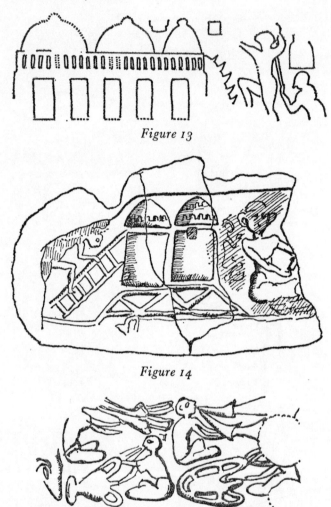

*Figure 13*

*Figure 14*

*Figure 15*

Arab geographers of early Islam condemn the Khuzians as ugly, uncouth, belligerent and greedy. Thousands of years earlier, the Assyrians and the Babylonians invariably referred to them as the 'wicked Elamites'. As far as the Sumerians were concerned, they were simply 'vandals', but at the same time weaklings. As the Sumerian proverb has it: 'When an Elamite is ill, his teeth chatter'; another proverb says: 'An Elamite is unhappy with nothing but a house to live in': in the opinion of the Sumerians, the Elamites were unreasonably presumptuous and avaricious.

But this is the view of their enemies, and so should be treated with caution. This much is certain: the Elamites were objects of deep suspicion to their Mesopotamian neighbours. Elam seemed to them to be a land of witches, magicians and evil spirits. Although a few shreds of evidence from their own country show the Elamites in a different light, furnishing above all heartening proof of a strong sense of family loyalty, even the modern scholar cannot help feeling that perhaps the Babylonians, the Assyrians and the Sumerians were not entirely mistaken.

The Elamites were unlike most other races. There was something in their character which made them difficult to understand fully, and in our investigation we shall encounter many remarkable and contradictory characteristics. On the one hand, they were governed by an imagination lively enough to invent the strangest fabulous creatures for their stone carvings (see Chapter VIII). On the other hand, they were of a saturnine and persevering disposition, intent upon immediate reality and avoiding anything superfluous – all this in addition to a basically pessimistic outlook. We have only to look at the terracotta head of an Elamite man from Susa (Plate 19), dating probably from the beginning of the first millennium B.C. André Parrot writes of it: 'This man's face is stern; his mouth is disapproving and without illusion.' Maurice Lambert describes the Elamites as: 'brutal, coarse, far too "canny" and far too "able" '. You would think they had never laughed.

But however sympathetically we may attempt to fathom the essentials of the Elamite character, we shall always find an insoluble enigma at its heart.

# CHAPTER II

# *Language and Script*

When, in 3000 B.C., the Sumerians invented a pictographic script as an aid to better book-keeping, the innovation was not slow to reach their Elamite neighbours. For soon afterwards, from Susa *Cb*, which corresponds to the stratum 'Uruk III' in Mesopotamia, (that is, 2900 B.C.), we find the first tablets in Elamite pictographs. Despite differences of detail it is nevertheless quite clear that the Elamite pictographs were based on the Sumerian pattern. It spread rapidly along the trade routes, and crops up almost simultaneously in the north-east, at Kashan (between Teheran and Isfahan), and in the far east, south of Kirman.

This so-called 'proto-Elamite' was, as in Sumeria, purely a pictographic script, both in its origins and for some time later. On the tablets we can recognize animals, jars, vases and similar objects. This script has not yet been deciphered, since many signs cannot be allotted an exact meaning and indeed will probably never be identified with certainty. However, the scholar is deprived of less than might appear at first glance, for the information in this script is confined to business – inventories, records of entry, receipts and delivery notes. Figure 16 provides an example. This tablet, which lists horses, is particularly informative, for it is the earliest occurrence of the

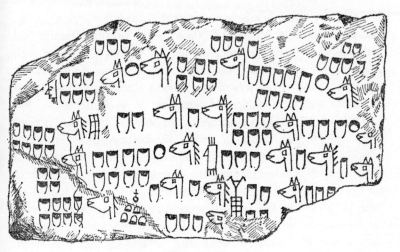

*Figure 16*

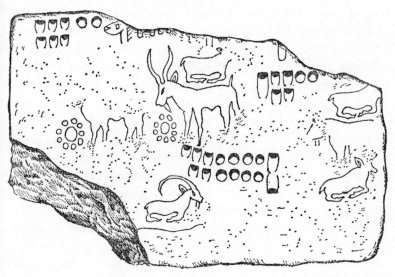

*Figure 17*

horse. Only their heads are represented, and according to the plausible view of V. Scheil, those with bristling manes are stallions, those with drooping manes are mares, and those with none at all are foals. The tablet also contains numbers, for example those to the left of the horses; thumb-like signs stand for units and little circles for tens, just as in Sumerian.

The proto-Elamite is, according to W. C. Brice, to be read from right to left. If this is correct, the bottom row (Figure 16) would end with 'mares : eight'. The signs that occur here and there next to a horse's head may denote the recipient or owner of the animal, and will therefore represent proper names or official titles. On the back (Figure 17) appears the total, 185, in the bottom centre : first at the far right the sign 'a hundred', to the left of that eight tens, and to the far left five units. Seal impressions of gazelles or chamois, some standing, some recumbent, show that the tablet was an official record; these seals may have belonged to the Royal Stud.

The proto-Elamite script probably contained barely more than 150 basic logograms, but they could of course be combined with each other in many ways, and this is why the tablets convey the false impression of a strikingly large array of signs. From this purely pictographic script there evolved a *syllabic* script; it contained only scattered examples of pictographs and developed, by a process of simplification, during the centuries after 2900 B.C. The development in Sumeria was similar; it seems likely that the scribal schools in both countries influenced each other. It was in this way that *linear script* arose in Elam and in Sumeria. It permitted not only the recording of trade negotiations, but also the expression of more intellectual matters—personal and political, historical and religious.

This Elamite linear script was probably established by the middle of the third millennium. However, it is only preserved for us from the twenty-third century, in six inscriptions on potsherds, eleven on stone, and one on a silver vase. No more seem to have been preserved.

At this final stage, the Elamite script seems to have contained about eighty symbols, of which fifty-five are so far recorded on stone. They commonly wrote from top to bottom, but occasionally the other way round. The lines sometimes being in the lefthand corner, but mostly in the right. Sometimes, the direction of the writing changes in the middle of a column, indicating a new paragraph. Because the signs of the Elamite linear script derive in part from the same pictographs as the Sumerian script, the two scripts have much in common, superficially at least. But they sound quite different, apart from the single sign *ki*, which is coincidental. For example, the Sumero-Babylonian sign *lum* is *shu* in Elamite, and so on.

All the surviving stone inscriptions in Elamite linear script date from one king, who ruled around 2250 B.C. Although they have lain in the Louvre since the turn of the century, they were only really deciphered in 1961. It is true that F. Bork asserted in 1905 that one of these stone inscriptions was the Elamite version of a Babylonian inscription above it or, to be precise, that the five-column Elamite inscription in Figure 18 was the translation of the lefthand column of the two Babylonian texts above it (omitted in the reproduction). Bork met only incredulity; but he was right. However, he was unable to prove his claim, and it is now evident that he was only able to identify three of the fifty-five signs correctly. And the efforts of C. Frank were also almost fruitless. The French scholars, to whom we are indebted for our knowledge, published it carefully in the form of photographs and copies, but when it came to deciphering it, they were no more successful than their German colleagues.

The deciphering of an unknown script is always an intellectual adventure, and I invite the reader to participate in it as far as possible. But first, I should like to tell a personal anecdote. In 1802, in Göttingen, G. F. Grotefend succeeded in deciphering the beginning of the ancient Persian cuneiform script of the great Kings Darius and Xerxes. When, in the summer of 1961, I had given a paper on my deciphering of the

Elamite linear script at the Orientalists' Symposium at Göttingen, one of the contributors told me that he had seen the name
'Grotefend' in large letters on a company building opposite the
conference hall, and that he had taken this to be a good omen.

Now, after this digression, let us attempt to retrace the path
of decipherment together. The first question is: Should the
signs in Figure 18 be read from top to bottom, or the other way
round?

Since, as you will remember, the Babylonian text is *above*
the Elamite one, we will assume that the Elamite columns are
to be read *from top to bottom*. At the bottom right in Figure
18, it seems as though space was insufficient; the fifth column
is much longer than the fourth. On the other hand, the middle
one is so short that it leads us to suppose that the scribe stopped
here because he had come to the end of a section. Working
from these assumptions, we decide to begin reading at the top
left, that is, at I/1, and to stop at the bottom right, at V/12.

Letting our eyes wander over the bewildering array of signs,
we find that columns I, II and III each contain a sign that
looks like the course of a river: in column I it is no. 7, in columns
II and III no. 5. And in each case it is followed by another sign
that looks like a trolley on its side: in column I no. 8, in columns
II and III no. 6. However, the 'trolley' in III/6 lacks one of its
lines, and is therefore not quite the same sign as in the other
two columns. So far, so good; but what can these signs mean?

We worked from the assumption that the Elamite inscription
was, as Bork thought, the translation of the lefthand column
of Babylonian script above it, which reads thus in English:

'To the god Inshushinak, his lord,
XY—shushinak,
Governor of Shusim [Susa], Regent of the land of Elam,
Son of Shimbishuk,
dedicated a bolt of bronze and cedar-wood'.

The basis for any further investigations lies in those *proper*

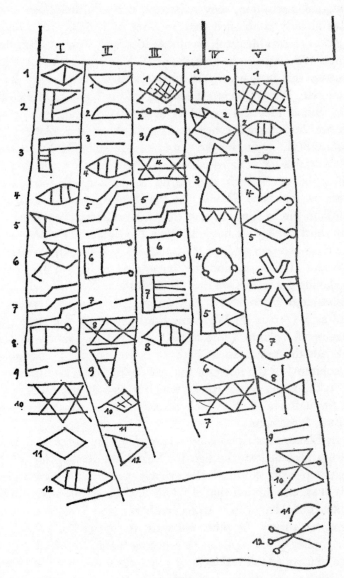

*Figure 18*

2—TLWOE * *

*names* that occur in the Babylonian text: just because it *is* a bilingual inscription, they must also occur in the Elamite. We have already established that, in three of the Elamite columns, a group of two identical, or almost identical, signs appears three times. We may also assume that each sign represents a syllable, because this is generally the case in Babylonian and also in Sumerian. We are therefore looking for three groups of identical – or almost identical – syllables in the Babylonian text. Where do we find them? Once in the name of the Elamite god *Inshushinak*, again in the name of the ruler X Y-*shushinak* (X Y stands for a Babylonian sign whose Elamite meaning has still to be ascertained), and thirdly in the name of the town of Susa, at that time *Shusim*. At that time it was not known as Shushim but as Shusim, and this small difference explains why our third 'trolley' is not quite like the others. In other words, the river-like sign at I/7, II/5 and III/5 is *shu*, the 'trolley' at I/8 and II/6 is *shi*, and the 'incomplete trolley' at III/6 is *si*.

Having got so far, we can fill in all the rest of the god's name Inshushinak in column I, thus: sign I/6 is *in*, sign I/9 is *na*, and sign I/10 is -*k*. We know that we are on the right track because in column I the signs 7–10 and in column II signs 5–8 are the same. So in both cases we can read –*shushinak*: in column I in the name of the god Inshushinak, and in column II in the name of the ruler – which is already partly known to us through the X Y, which stands for the Babylonian word *puzur*: 'protection'.

In Elamite inscriptions of a later date, the name of a god is always preceded by the sign for 'deity', in Elamite *nap*. So the next step is to substitute the syllable *nap* for the sign at I/5; this is an assumption that F. Bork and C. Frank have already made. But what next? Armed with our new knowledge of the signs, we survey the other columns. At the top of column IV our 'trolley' – the sign for *shi* – occurs again, and under it the sign that we established as *in* at I/6. And so the word in column IV begins with *shi-in-*, and ends with the trellis-like sign (IV/7) which we have already come across at I/10 and II/8, and which we decided was -*k*. Therefore column IV begins with *shi-in-*, and ends with -*k*.

And now we have come to a cross-roads, for it is plain that if, at the outset, you put in even one wrong sign, you are doomed to failure. So far we have only established seven signs, and so are still at the beginning; on our next decisions hang the success or failure of our deciphering.

Let us consult the Babylonian text once more. Perhaps we may find in it a proper name which begins with *shi-in-* and ends with -*k*. And in fact we do : the name of the father of our ruler Shimbishhuk in the Babylonian spelling. In reality, this Elamite, of whom we know nothing more, was called *Shinpi-hish-huk*, in accordance with Elamite grammar and vocabulary; this probably meant : 'His name was dedicated to the snake.' For, as I shall show in Chapter III, the Elamites had a special veneration for snakes, and so there is nothing surprising in such a name. Indeed, many of our inscriptions are found on or near stone-carved snakes.

Now we only have to fit this name Shinpi-hish-huk into Column IV. We proceed thus : at IV/1 *shi* as we already know; at IV/2 *in* as we know too; at IV/3 *pi*; at IV/4 (a circle with three dots) *hi*; at IV/5 *ish*; at IV/6 (a diamond) *hu*; and at IV/7, as we know, -*k,* thus *shi-in-pi-hi-ish-hu-k* – Shinpi-hish-huk.

Next, let us look at the middle column. In it we found the name of the town of Susa (Shusim in ancient Elamite). In passing, we can now identify the sign at III/7 as the syllable *im*, and so *shu-si-im* is the same as Shusim/Susa. According to the Babylonian text we would expect the Elamite title of 'land-regent' to precede it. From later cuneiform sources we know that to be *hal-menik* (*hal* land, *menik* regent). Reassured, we replace the sign III/1 by *hal*, the sign at III/2 (a chain) by *me*, III/3 (a curve) by *ni*, and III/4 – but we know it already, for it is our trellis-like sign -*k* from I/10, II/8, and IV/7. Further, this *k* is exactly where it should be to make *hal-menik*, land-regent. At last we feel firm ground beneath our feet ...

We have now identified fifteen signs altogether, less than a third of the extant *fifty-five*. Armed with this, we shall have comparatively little trouble with the remaining two-thirds. However, since our supply of proper names is exhausted, any further work must be based on a knowledge of the Elamite language; I must therefore confine myself to reporting the results of my investigation. From my own knowledge I was able to identify the name of the author of the inscription as *Kutik-Inshushinak*, meaning 'He who is protected by the god Inshushinak'. In its entirety, the inscription in Figure 18 reads thus, written out and translated into English:

I    te-im-tik-ki nap in-shu-shi-na-k nu-ki
II   u ku-tu-ki-shu-shi-na-k zunkik hal-me ak?
III  hal-me-ni-k shu-si-im-ki
IV   shi-in-pi-hi-ish-hu-k
V    sha-ki-ri nap-ir lik hi-an ti-la-ni-li


I    To the lord god Inshushinak have this wood (-bolt)
II   I, Kutik-Inshushinak, king of the land,
III  Land-regent of Susa,
IV   Shinpi-hish-huk's
V    son, (given) to the deity as an offering to the temple.

Unfortunately, the Elamite linear script died out around 2220 B.C. with Kutik-Inshushinak, the ruler referred to above. Eventually it was replaced by the Sumerian-Babylonian (Akkadian) script, which finally developed into the well-known cuneiform. Its influence on Elam had already begun in the twenty-fourth or even the twenty-fifth century B.C., as is shown by the fragment of an inscription from Liyan (at Bushire in the Persian Gulf), the oldest source of this type (Figure 19). And yet, even this tiny fragment of Elamite text in Akkadian linear script betrays certain stylistic peculiarities in the formation of the signs. The Liyan scribes, therefore, adapted unhesitatingly whatever they had gleaned from abroad to suit their own tastes

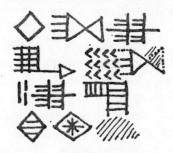

*Figure 19*

– typically Elamite behaviour, one is tempted to add. Thereafter, up till the decline of the kingdom in 640 B.C., the
Akkadian cuneiform script was invariably given highly idiosyncratic treatment by the Elamites; it can be seen above all in
the ways the Elamite scribal schools handled what they borrowed from Mesopotamia.

As the extinct native linear script had consisted almost
entirely of syllables, they considered that the Akkadian script
should also be syllabic as far as possible. And so the Elamite
scribes threw overboard the whole tedious ballast of logograms
and such ambiguities which their Mesopotamian colleagues
piously preserved as part of the Sumerian heritage. In a deliber-
ate and rational manner – this too is an Elamite characteristic
– the scribes at Susa exploited all possibilities of the foreign
cuneiform; they simplified it and led it to the threshold of
alphabetic script. Of course, they never crossed this threshold,
not even when, in about 520 B.C., they collaborated dutifully
with Aramaic secretaries to invent the ancient Persian cuneiform for King Darius, which became a compromise between a
cuneiform and an alphabetic script.

Darius the Great (522–486) had almost all his inscriptions
written in the three main languages of his empire, that is, in
ancient Persian, Elamite and Babylonian. This is why the way
lay open to Western scholars for decipherment of the cuneiform
script. A pioneer in this field was Georg Friedrich Grotefend

(1775–1853), referred to above, who taught Greek at Göttingen grammar school.

In a paper of 4 September 1802, he managed to identify correctly ten of the signs of ancient Persian cuneiform. And he had already realized that the Elamite cuneiform had also to be read from left to right. In 1837 he discovered that, before proper names and before certain other important words in Elamite, a vertical mark stood as an 'indicator'; technically this is known as a 'determinative'. He also discovered the symbol for 'king'.

Other nineteenth-century pioneers in deciphering Elamite cuneiform were N. L. Westergaard, E. Hincks, H. C. Rawlinson, E. Norris and J. Oppert. F. H. Weissbach brought their work to a provisional conclusion, and since then only a few isolated signs have been discovered, principally in the Elamite tablets from Darius's treasury and court administration at Persepolis. This is because the Achaemenids entrusted their official records to Elamite scribes up to 460 B.C., the time of Artaxerxes I. In 1911 F. H. Weissbach counted 113 later Elamite signs, and even today we only know of 10 more, discovered by G. G. Cameron and R. T. Hallock. In Early and Middle Elamite periods there had been 174 syllabic symbols and about 25 word symbols (logograms). Since, in the course of one and a half centuries, it has been possible to connect nearly all the Elamite cuneiform signs with their Akkadian originals, and thus to establish their phonetic value, Elamite inscriptions and tablets can on the whole be deciphered without too much difficulty, as long as they are in good condition. However, it is not enough just to be able to *read* the texts; we are still ill-equipped to understand them.

The only firm basis is to be found in the Elamite vocabulary which was established for us in the trilingual inscriptions of the ancient Persian kings, above all of Darius and Xerxes, and which comprises in all about seven hundred words. Anything more must be wrested from the text by unremitting combination, comparison, and indeed by guesswork. In this some scholars have given their imagination too free a rein and thus became entangled in pernicious snares. Elamite inscriptions exist in which every second word poses a problem; sometimes we do not really understand a whole sentence.

This state of affairs has dissuaded many cuneiform scholars from studying the Elamite language. Everybody's hopes are pinned on the possibility that some time, out of the rubble of centuries, there might emerge an Elamite-Akkadian word-list. Certainly, such 'vocabularies' must have existed in the scribal schools of Elam and Mesopotamia, but so far archaeologists have been blessed with no such find.

Fundamentally, the Akkadian cuneiform was not ill-suited to the Elamite language. This was because Elamite possessed, among other peculiarities, such as an addiction to nasals, many and various consonant clusters, which a syllabic script is basically ill-adapted to reproduce. To quote an example : what is written in cuneiform as *te-ip-ti and te-im-ti* is an attempt to represent what is really *tempt*, 'a lord'. Further, this *tempt* was so heavily nasalized that the Assyrians thought they were hearing just *te* from the Elamites. Thus they write the name of the Elamite King *Tempt-Humban* simply as *Te-Umman*.

It is only with the greatest difficulty that we are able to trace, here and there beneath the surface of the cuneiform script, the peculiar timbre of Elamite. As far as the pronunciation is concerned, there is sometimes hardly any difference between *d* and *t*, between *b* and *p*, or even between *g* and *k*. Nor were the Elamite scribes always consistent, even in the same word : 'I gave' was sometimes written *du-ni-h*, sometimes *tu-ni-h*. And so it is not from them that we can discover whether the voiced or the unvoiced pronunciation was preferred; the answer is to a certain extent to be found among Elam's neighbours. According to the way in which the Assyrians and the Babylonians reproduced Elamite proper names or technical expressions, the evidence seems to be that they heard soft consonants. (We may find a parallel in the present-day dialect of Saxony.)

As one would expect from the obstinate character of the Elamite people, their language remained surprisingly constant over the centuries. As long as we remember the phonetic development of the early *u* to the later *i* (by means of an intermediate *ü*), it is not difficult to link Early Elamite to Late by way of Middle Elamite.

# CHAPTER III

# *Religion*

If we possessed an exact knowledge of the religious world of the Elamites and of the religious observances which it exacted, we should approach an understanding of the Elamites themselves. For even the scanty sources available to us bear witness to the overwhelming role that religion played in their life.

It is true that this religion displays many traits connecting it with the customs of neighbouring Mesopotamia; essentially, however, Elamite religion remains ineffaceably individual and idiosyncratic. Part of this individuality consists in an uncommon reverence and respect for eternal womanhood, and in a worship of snakes that has its roots in magic; the snake is, as I have already said, a true *leitmotif* of Elamite civilization.

Even the pottery of the third and fourth millennia swarms with snakes (Plate 20). They appear on jar-stoppers and on the lids of vessels as symbols of protection against evil. Snakes rear up as guardians of the gates, crawl over carvings of kings (Plate 30), twine round altar plates or form the handles of *ex votos* such as axes, sceptres and the like. Coiled up, they serve as a seat for the god (Figure 23; Plates 5 and 6). Since ancient times, the motif of the snake round the tree of life has been represented in Elam, and the Elamite fertility symbol of two snakes mating penetrated as far as Egypt. Snakes with human heads (Figure 20) provide evidence of the deification

*Figure 20*

of these reptiles, a deification of a type unknown in Mesopotamia.

As with the language, so the religion of Elam betrays a sense of purpose that survived many centuries. In the very earliest Elamite text that has been preserved, a treaty dating from around 2280 B.C. (Plate 21), we find almost all the gods who belonged to the Elamite pantheon when the kingdom was overthrown in 640 B.C. And even when they first emerge into the limelight of history, they make their appearance as a firmly established hierarchy, which indicates that the world of the gods was already extremely old in the twenty-third century.

Pride of place in this world was taken by a *goddess* – and this is typical of Elam. The treaty we have mentioned opens with the following appeal : 'Hear, Goddess Pinikir, and you good gods of heaven!' Later, too, the Elamites saw Pinikir as the mistress of heaven endowed with the power to curse, and her name often forms a part of proper names. Thus, a daughter of the most famous Elamite King, Shilhak-Inshushinak, was called Utu-e-hihhi-Pinikir, which probably means : 'I have dedicated her womb to Pinikir.' The Mesopotamians saw Pinikir as a kind of Ishtar, the Biblical Astarte. She was clearly the 'great mother of the gods' to the Elamites. The very fact that precedence was given to a goddess, who stood above and apart from the other Elamite gods, indicates a matriarchal approach in the devotees of this religion.

There was, however, another such mother of the gods in the

far south-east, in the coastal region of the Persian Gulf. She was called *Kiririsha*, and the home of her cult was at Liyan – at Bushire. Incidentally, Kiririsha is not a proper name in origin, but an epithet which means 'great goddess' (*kiri*, goddess', and *risha*, 'great'). Kiririsha gradually penetrated from Liyan to the north-west, for Middle and Late Elamite kings and princes dedicated temples to her in Susiana. In the capital of Susa itself, Kiririsha enjoyed the proud title of 'Mother of the gods' and 'Mistress of the high temple'. However, Kiririsha was never confused with Pinikir, native to Susa as she was.

But these are not all. In 710 B.C. Prince Hanne in Ayapir, or Izeh, called on Parti as well as Kiririsha, and worshipped her as the 'Good mother of the gods'. This confusion about the mother of the gods can be explained by the historical development of Elam, and reflects the federal constitution of the country. In the oldest times each large area of Elam must have possessed its own mother of the gods: Susiana had Pinikir, who probably originated from the mountains to the north; Kiririsha was the mother of the southern coastal region by the Persian Gulf; and the Eastern mountains of Anshan had Parti.

Strangely enough, the Elamites were not in the least disturbed by having two or three mothers of the gods. It is true that the influence of Kiririsha was felt throughout Elam during the second millennium; simultaneously, however, the locally established mother of the gods remained unchallenged. The Elamites prudently made individual votive offerings to both the domestic and the alien goddesses, dedicating separate gifts to them. In any case, they do not seem to have honoured more than two mothers of the gods in the same place, except perhaps in Susa, where in the later period of the kingdom, in addition to Pinikir and Kiririsha, Parti is also acknowledged.

In the third millennium, these 'great mothers of the gods' still held undisputed sway at the head of the Elamite pantheon, but a change came during the course of the second. Just as the age-old matriarchy of Elam had once yielded in the face of a gradual rise in the position of men (see Chapter V), so a

*Figure 21*

corresponding rearrangement took place among the gods. Not without a struggle, the mother of the gods, be she Pinikir or Kiririsha, abdicated in favour of a male deity. Yet she was never excluded from the élite of the Elamite pantheon, for she held a permanent place in the hearts of the simple folk. This is proved by the countless clay figures of the so-called 'naked' goddess which have emerged from the rubble; they represent her holding her breasts with both hands (Figure 21), and are probably intended to be Pinikir or Kiririsha.

The male deity to whom the 'great goddess' was forced to relinquish her position was *Humban*. During the third millennium he still occupied the third place, but from the middle of the second millennium he stood at the head of the pantheon. In contrast to the mothers of the gods, with their local allegiances, he was always worshipped throughout Elam. Under the title of 'Master of heaven' he was, in Susa, husband to the 'Mistress of heaven' – Pinikir initially and later Kiririsha, who actually bore the title of 'Great wife'. This second marriage resulted in the birth of the god *Hutran*. In the catalogue of the gods that occurs in the treaty of 2280 B.C., Hutran is admittedly placed only fifteenth of the thirty-seven deities, but he was still known to the Assyrians in the seventh century under the name of *Uduran* – the initial H is silent and the *t* is voiced.

Humban's rivals for the position at the head of the gods were, above all, the great city gods. Due to the rise of Susa from a mere provincial town in the third millennium to its position as the capital city of the kingdom of Elam in the second, the god of Susa inevitably became prominent; his name, *Inshushinak*, was developed from the Sumerian *Nin-shushin-ak*, 'Lord of Susa', most likely at a period when Susa was under the sway of the Sumerians. As late as 2260 B.C., Inshushinak had only attained sixth position out of the thirty-seven deities. One millennium later, however, he, Humban and Kiririsha compose a firmly established trinity at the head of the Elamite pantheon. In inscriptions, the order of precedence is usually Humban, Kiririsha and then Inshushinak, but occasionally Inshushinak replaces Kiririsha in second place after Humban. He never achieved complete supremacy.

In the course of his rise, Inshushinak's titles became increasingly more imposing. From the very beginning, the ordinary people had invoked him as a 'Father of the weak', a mode of address that exudes a deep affection. In the early Babylonian period, that is, in the first half of the second millennium, one Elamite ruler describes Inshushinak the god as his 'king', and another as 'King of the gods'. This title implies that Inshushinak had reached the top, and this is consistent with a thirteenth-century source which describes both Humban and Inshushinak as 'King of the gods'. Every subsequent ruler designated himself as 'The beloved servant of Inshushinak', and the titles that the god was given reached the summit of splendour under Shilhak-Inshushinak during the twelfth century. This king saw him as the 'Great lord, the lord of my capital, benefactor of the high temple, all-faithful protector who gave us his name'. Even in the eighth century, he was worshipped as 'Protector of the gods of heaven and of the earth'.

45

In a text which invokes the triple constellation of the gods Humban, Inshushinak and Kiririsha, the latter is expressly described as a 'Great wife'. We can deduce from this that Kiririsha, in her capacity as mother of the gods, had as husband not only Humban but also Inshushinak. Indeed, it seems probable that the three deities were considered as siblings, for similar relationships clearly existed throughout the history of the ruling houses of Elam; two brothers would take their sister to wife, although not simultaneously. Relationships between the gods who composed the highest trinity must simply have been modelled on those established on the terrestrial level by the confined circle of the royal family.

As we see it today, it appears that, among all the gods, it was Inshushinak who wielded the greatest influence over the moods of the Elamites; for the religious inscriptions, usually so formal and so stiff, suddenly come to life as soon as Inshushinak appears on the scene. And so King Untash-napirisha, who was responsible for erecting thousands of monotonously similar votive texts on the wall friezes of his ziggurat at Choga Zambil, appeals to him in these very human and touching words: 'May it please the god Inshushinak to approach, to grant us his gifts, and to speak [his words].' Even the man who annihilated Elam, the Assyrian King Assurbanipal, describes Inshushinak as 'The mysterious god who lingers in a secret place where no one can see what his divine being is about'.

In the course of a search for the causes of this uneasy awe towards Inshushinak, an attitude which would be incomprehensible were he no more than the city god of Susa, one is struck by his close connections with the goddess *Ishnikarab*. Together with her, Inshushinak became the god of oaths by whom one swore throughout the whole of Elam: in all kinds of legislation, oaths during trials were sworn on Inshushinak and Ishnikarab. At the beginning of the second millennium, the goddess was still called *Ishmekarab*; this is good Akkadian and means 'She has granted our prayers.' And so it is likely that this goddess first made her way into Elam under Akkadian influence. Once there, she acquired sanctuary – permanent sanctuary what is more, not like the foreign gods Nergal, Enki (or Ea), Ninegal, Anunitum, Adad, Nabû, Nusku and Shala, who were only temporarily accepted as part of the Elamite pantheon.

However, the particular part that Ishnikarab played has only become clear since an unusual discovery in Susa brought to light burial tablets dating from the first millennium B.C. It emerges from them that Ishnikarab, as well as the goddess *Lagamal* (*Lagamar*), received the departed in the underworld. In one tablet their souls are described thus: 'They have entered upon the path and are going their way. Ishnikarab and Lagamal are coming towards them . . . In the grave Inshushinak imparts his judgment to them.'

This then is the key to Inshushinak's mysterious power: he rules the kingdom of the dead. And now we also understand why his name is linked with Ishnikarab's in the oaths of the living: Ishnikarab is his closest helper in the other world, the world where judgement is made. The connection between Inshushinak and Ishnikarab can also be deduced indirectly from the inscription of King Untash-napirisha referred to above. It is true that it is Inshushinak whom the ruler implores with gifts to appear and to speak. But in spite of this, the offering on which the inscription is to be found – a blue-glazed terracotta pommel – is dedicated not to Inshushinak but to Ishnikarab. It appears that during the early Babylonian period, Inshushinak slowly succeeded in ousting Nergal, the Sumerian god of the underworld, and establishing himself as ruler of the Elamite underworld. It is also significant in this connection that the witnesses in Elamite legal texts are almost invariably introduced by two deities, the sun-god and Inshushinak. Thus, these two were considered as the lords of light and darkness, and so as lords of the earth and of the kingdom of the dead.

Elam's sun-god was called *Nahhunte*, which is also the native

word for 'sun', originally *nan-hunde*, that is, 'creator of the day'.
Nahhunte was the special god of the execution of the law, and
we shall discuss him further in this capacity in Chapter V. In
the treaty of 2280 B.C. the sun-god occupies fifth place, above
Inshushinak. The following words are reiterated in it: 'A
king is the faithful servant of Nahhunte; a king is subject to
Inshushinak.' This also emphasizes the dual role of the gods
who represent the law: as long as men, even kings, walk in
terrestrial light, their loyalties are due to the sun-god; but once
they have reached the kingdom of shadows, they become the
subjects of Inshushinak, judge of the dead.

Besides the sun-god, there was also always a moon-god in
Elam; indeed, all the constellations were deified by the
Elamites, as were the natural forces and even the sea. Unfortunately the name of the moon-god was almost invariably
transcribed by the Akkadian logogram s i n (moon), so that his
Elamite name has not yet been definitely established. He was
probably known as *Napir*, because this god is surnamed 'the
shining'. For the Elamites, the moon-god was above all considered as the 'father of orphans'.

I will only mention the most important of the countless other
Elamite gods. Of these, *Simut* (*Shimut*) is outstanding; he
bears the remarkable title of the 'God of the Elamites'. He was
seen as the 'strong herald of the gods', and was clearly honoured
throughout the country. His wife was *Manzat* (*Manzit*); I
mentioned her briefly in the Introduction in connection with
her temple at Hupshen (Deh-e-nou). In the treaty of 2280 B.C.,
in which Simut occupies the seventh place, directly below
Inshushinak, Manzat was only allotted the eighteenth, below
*Siyashum* but above *Narunte*.

These latter goddesses stand as sisters to the 'great mother
goddess'. Siyashum seems to have been protectress of the palace
of the gods, but Narunte soon gained a reputation as goddess
of victory. King Kutik-Inshushinak, whom we met in Chapter
II in connection with the decipherment of the Elamite linear
script, specially dedicated a temple to Narunte in Susa; her

limestone statue, 81 centimetres high, is now in the Louvre (Plate 4). Her dedicator addresses her thus in Akkadian : 'Bend your ear to my pleading! Preserve me my right!' The goddess, clad in a pleated robe, is seated barefoot on a throne decorated with six heraldic lions; her missing head was found lately. With her right hand, Narunte seems to be holding a bowl for libations, with her left, perhaps a palm-fan. The Elamite inscription made by King Kutik-Inshushinak, in his native linear script, can be seen on the corner of the throne, the left-hand one in the reproduction, with a short column running across the bottom of the throne. If my translation is correct, it means : 'The victory was achieved through Narunte.' During the early Babylonian period, about five hundred years later, it is not uncommon in Susa to find women's names like *Narunte-ummi* (in Akkadian, 'Narunte is mother to me'); thus Narunte was not only the goddess of victory. It must be admitted that her reputation in Mesopotamia was not so high – indeed, a late Assyrian catalogue of the gods describes her as sister of the 'evil seven'.

Other Elamite deities, such as the river-god *Shazi*, who was appealed to during trials as the judge of ordeals, will also be mentioned later.

We can only form a vague idea of how the Elamites conceived of divinity and approached the powers above. It is certain that they considered all worldly goods as gifts of the gods; we learn this, rather unexpectedly, from the otherwise arid legal sources dating from the Early Babylonian period in Susa. In these texts we find an account of all imaginable resources – fields, meadows, buildings, gardens, corn, silver, and so on – with the illuminating remark : 'In short, everything that the godhead has given to men as their own'.

The Elamites were convinced that all the gods possessed a mysterious and supernatural power expressed by the word *kiten*; this word was adopted into the Akkadian from Elamite in the form *kidennu*. From the way it is written in Akkadian, we can infer that the Elamites must have pronounced it *kidenn,* with the *t* voiced and with the accent on the second syllable. This *kiten* was the magical charm, the aura of divinity and its power to protect – but also to chastise. W. F. Leemans realized that it could take physical shape as a taboo emblem in bronze or stone. The rulers of Elam founded their domination on the magical protection of the *kiten* – the king's attitude towards his subjects was that of an earthly representative of the divine *kiten*. He who violated it forfeited his life, 'lost his peace', and had to die (see Chapter V). While all the gods possessed this *kiten*, Humban's was considered to be the special charisma of the rulers, at any rate after he reached the pinnacle of the Elamite pantheon.

Our only information on the religious observances of the Elamites is derived from a few isolated finds. Among the countless early seals, with the varied scenes they show, there is so far only one that deals with an act of worship, and that in a strangely irreverent fashion (Figure 22). The figure of a god is being borne in procession through the town on a litter; a musician is seated in front of the statue; alongside walk men, one of whom is wearing a strange kind of hat. They are carry-

*Figure 22*

ing standards and symbolical objects, and also peculiar ropes, which may be intended to represent snakes.

Religious processions bearing statues of the gods were also common throughout Mesopotamia, but these 'rallies' had a flavour that was peculiarly Elamite; the faithful, led by priests and dignitaries, perhaps even by the royal family, would set forth on a pilgrimage to a holy place (Plate 7). There stood cult statues and altars, sacrifices were made and prayers offered to the gods. The favoured destinations of such pilgrimages were high places, either a high temple in the town or a shrine on a mountain ridge, far out in the country.

Such in its austere grandeur is the shrine that has been preserved at the hamlet of Setolan, between Basht and Nura-bad, and thus in the middle of Anshan. This monument at Kurangan (in the local dialect, *Kurangun*) has been hewn out of a rocky mountain peak, high above the river Fahlian (Plate 5). The details of the rock relief, smooth and much weather-beaten, can be made out in the sketch provided by its dis-coverer, Ernst Herzfeld (Figure 23). On it, we see a procession of the devout; originally they probably numbered about forty, but in the course of centuries many have crumbled away and rolled down the cliff-face. According to L. Vanden Berghe, this section on the left dates only from the eighth century B.C.

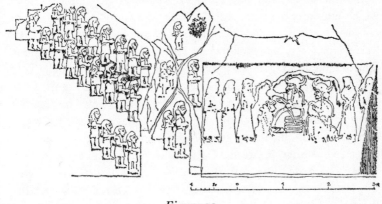

*Figure 23*

The procession makes its way down steps towards the narrow platform; the main relief, which stands above this platform, may be attributed to 2000 B.C. The priests who used to sacrifice in front of it needed a good head for heights if they were to avoid the danger of toppling over the precipice into the Fahlian below. On the long side of the platform there are the reliefs of two gods, identifiable by the horns on their crowns. One is a male deity with a long beard – probably Humban – and his throne is formed by a coiled-up snake; the god grasps its head with his left hand. Behind him in the drawing, but probably intended to be next to him, sits a goddess, perhaps Kiririsha or Parti.

A similar representation is to be found still deeper into Anshan, on the rock of Naqsh-e-Rostam, not far from Persepolis in southern Iran (Plate 6). In it, the Sassanid King Bahram II has had images of himself and his council superimposed on an Elamite relief. Of the original monument we can still make out, on the far right, an Elamite dignitary, and, between him and the king, the traces of two snake thrones. In any case, the Elamite relief at Naqsh-e-Rostam is probably, on the evidence of the clothing – cape and hood – more than a millennium later than the one from Kurangan which also shows a snake throne.

On the latter, the god is holding in his right hand a vessel which contains the water of life. This idea – and that of horned crowns for the gods – has clearly been borrowed from the Sumerians. The water flows to left and right, and two male figures clad in long robes receive it; they may represent the king and his brother. They are each followed by the figure of a woman, whose clothes reach to the ground; and on the left there is another male figure. It is likely that all five are to be thought of as a single group, standing *in front of* the two deities, or rather in front of the altar which has been erected before the gods. The devout, who have made their way to the shrine and who now descend the steps, are considerably smaller than the figures on the platform, except for the two pilgrim leaders, who are of medium height. Apart from the first one none of them has a beard and they all wear their hair in a long plait. The Elamites seem to have been fond of plaits at all periods; Prince Hanne, for example, in Plate 18, is wearing his hair in two plaits, exactly the same way as did the eighteenth-century anonymous Elamite king (Plate 27), roughly a thousand years earlier.

The participants in Elamite worship were clearly familiar with two different attitudes of prayer, that of 'address' and that of 'silence'. The former consisted of stretching both hands up in the presence of the deity; probably a prayer was said at the same time. This attitude is adopted by those praying on the platform in the relief at Kurangan. If the faithful one were bringing an offering at the same time, he only raised his right hand (Plates 24 and 25). The 'silent' attitude can be seen among the congregation on the steps; their hands are crossed over their belts. The same position of silent devotion is to be seen in the rock reliefs of Hanne, with his wife and son, in the gorge of Salman at Izeh (Plate 18) and – portrayed with particular solemnity – in the bronze statue from Susa of Queen Napir-asu (Plate 29).

The regular acts of worship of the Elamites – as distinct from pilgrimages – took place in those temples and shrines which are so amply recorded in inscriptions; it is unfortunate that no such shrine has been preserved. The largest site of this type is the ziggurat which King Untash-napirisha dedicated in the thirteenth century, together with the town of Al-Untash (or Dur-Untash, now Choga Zambil). As I mentioned in the Introduction, its vast remains have now been exposed (Plates 8–13). As it is one of the most impressive examples of Elamite architectural skill, I shall describe this ziggurat at Choga Zambil more thoroughly in Chapter VIII; here it is only a question of tracing the pervading characteristics of Elamite religion as they are reflected in quite general form in the construction of the temple.

*The Lost World of Elam*

It is fortunate that in the course of uncovering Choga Zambil, such typical sites have also been discovered; until then not even one single Elamite temple foundation was known to us. In Plate 8, a view taken from the top of the ziggurat towards the north, we can see the remains of three temples between the internal and the external fortifications; in the left foreground, immediately behind the north gate of the inner wall, there is a temple to Humban; in the right at the middle of the picture there is a site dedicated to the two gods Hishmitik and Ruhurater (members of the pantheon in the mountains of Anshan). In the background, the Diz flows peacefully through the desert.

In the eastern corner of the sacred precinct known as the *Siyankuk* (Figure 24), the French archaeological mission in Choga Zambil uncovered particularly informative temple foundations. Only the building which appears at the top in the sketch falls outside the general plan. This belonged to the group of gods known as the *Napratep* which consisted of four pairs of deities; this can be deduced from the double pedestals which stand in four niches on the back wall of the building. *Nap* is the Elamite word for 'deity', whilst *ratep* means 'nourishing' (in the plural form); thus *napratep* denotes – possibly female – 'nourishing godheads'.

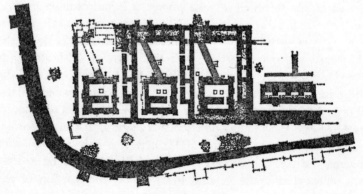

*Figure 24*

The foundations of the other three temples in Figure 24 are identical. Going from bottom to top, they are consecrated to Pinikir, the ancient mother-goddess of Susa; to the two Babylonian gods Adad and Ninali, the weather-god and his wife; and to the two Elamite gods Simut and Manzat. At all three sites the temple area is enclosed by a rectangular wall, and the only entrance is afforded by a gate on the right in the south-western wall. From here a path paved with large square bricks leads past a sacrificial table and approaches the entrance gate in the middle of the temple façade *at an angle*. It seems that as a matter of principle the Elamites approached their shrines not directly from the front but obliquely. For example, not one of the seven wall gates at Choga Zambil, nor one of the paths, leads straight to the portals of the ziggurat: it would have seemed irreverent. In each of the three shrines in Figure 24 there are two rooms. In the first, which was rectangular, stood the statue or statues of the gods; in the temple of Pinikir there is one pedestal, in the other two there are two. On the lefthand side, a narrow door led to a second room, long and narrow; its purpose remains unknown. To each site was attached a row of four cells in the forecourt along the left surrounding wall, which would probably have housed priests, temple servants and utensils.

The entrances of Elamite temples were guarded by statues of lions, bulls or gryphons. There was no need for such statues to be of enormous size, for it is clear that the *kiten* alone, the magical power of these statues, was considered sufficient to protect the shrines. In Choga Zambil, or example, terracotta bulls encrusted with blue lapis lazuli were found among the rubble in the temples of Adad and Ninali; if their size were the only guide, they would seem more like bull-calves. We have unexpected evidence of this from Assurbanipal in his account of the overthrow of Susa: 'I tore out the wild bulls, the adornment of the (temple)-doors.'

Our only information on the *shape* of Elamite temples is to be found in seal-rolls from the early period and in a carving

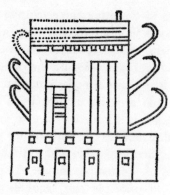

*Figure 25*

from Nineveh of the late Assyrian period. In Figure 25, from
a seal of the third millennium B.C., the temple in ancient Elam
is shown as a fairly high square building on a terraced foundation; the brickwork on the façade was apparently adorned
with niches; behind it, steps may have provided side access to
the temple. On the temple itself we can see two high door-
frames, of which only the lefthand one was actually used as an
entrance – a reed curtain partially protects it against the sun –
while the one on the right may have been just a false door.
The temple roof was flat, composed of several rows of wooden
beams. The interior was lit and ventilated by a row of small
square windows between the doors and the roof.

The most striking feature of the temple is three huge horns
projecting from the wall on both sides, and this brings us to
a peculiarity of Elamite temple construction that we have until
now ignored. Middle Elamite inscriptions prove that these
horns (*e-ul*) formed an important part of every temple, as they
were a symbol of divinity. Indeed, King Shilhak-Inshushinak
boasted in the twelfth century that he had restored twenty
'horn-temples'. Five hundred years later, Assurbanipal informs
us proudly that, in the course of his conquest of Susa, he has
had the 'horns of cast bronze' hacked from the ziggurat. A carving from his royal palace at Nineveh (now Mossul) portrays

the high temple of this very ziggurat at Susa with two huge pairs of horns at the front (Figure 33).

As regards the *internal* arrangements of Elamite temples our knowledge from excavations is scanty, because everything of any value was pillaged years ago. However, some idea of the riches that filled the temples is afforded by the dedicatory texts and by occasional finds bearing religious inscriptions. The majority of the finds are statues of iron, stone or glazed clay; they represent not only various deities and protective spirits, but also kings, together with the countless members of their families. Victorious Elamite kings set up captured stelae before their favourite god Inshushinak. For his part, Assurbanipal claims to have dragged off thirty-two Elamite statues of kings, cast in gold, silver or bronze, or carved in alabaster.

The temple was also furnished with altars and sacrificial tables, on many of which we can still make out the drainage runnels for the sacrificial blood and for libations. All kinds of utensils and offerings stood on the altars and daises or hung on the walls : statues of animals – sheep, goats, tortoises, and many others – in wood, bronze, or stone; taboo emblems of the god; and weapons of all kinds such as swords, axes and arrows. But one problem remains unsolved : the purpose of the glazed clay pommels, inscribed with the name of King Untash-napirisha; he had them buried in their hundreds in chambers in the ziggurat at Choga Zambil, left empty for this purpose.

To the temple offerings which were dedicated by rulers and potentates, we must add the huge numbers of offerings from the Elamite populace. They include amulets, ornaments of all kinds, and also simple clay cones bearing religious inscriptions, one of which can be seen in Figure 26. It is only six centimetres high, but there is room for two lines of the early Elamite linear script which – as I have said – became obsolete about 2220 B.C. Half of the inscription is still unclear, but the end of the other line may mean : 'May the king of the land be protected, may he be protected.' It is clear that some worthy subject is attempting here to incline the gods favourably towards his lord.

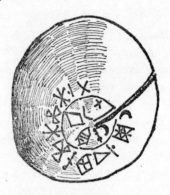

*Figure 26*

The last, but by no means the least, peculiarity of Elamite temples was their *sacred groves*. They are mentioned in inscriptions, for example in the temple of the sun-god Nahhunte at Susa and of the goddess Kiririsha at Dur-Untash, and were probably an essential part of every Elamite temple. This is the report of Assurbanipal when he overthrew Susa: 'I have razed the temple of Elam. I made her gods and goddesses as the wind. My soldiers penetrated her secret grove, where no stranger has ever trodden or even been to the edge; they saw its secrets and destroyed them by fire . . .'

You realize the implications of maintaining the sacred grove in the temple of the capital of Susa when you see how difficult it is, even nowadays, to provide the French mission up on the ruins of the original capital with daily water supplies. In those days, long donkey-trains trooped up to the temple and back to the river innumerable times; each animal bore two goatskins of water from the Ulai. For the sacred groves were by no means miniature gardens; we are told that on one occasion ten trees were felled in the shrine of the goddess Simut at Susa alone. Nor was water needed only for the sacred groves, but also for the priests, above all for the ritual ablutions and libations, to say nothing of the water needed for the general upkeep of the temple.

Sources only afford us an occasional glimpse of the religious *practices* of the Elamites. Worship was generally accompanied by music. On the seal in Figure 22, a musician can be seen seated in front of the statue while it was paraded through the streets. In 2250 B.C., King Kutik-Inshushinak paid musicians to sing and play to him morning and evening in front of the main entrance to the temple which he had dedicated to Inshushinak. One and a half millennia later, we come across musicians on the carving of Prince Hanne in the gorge at Kul-e Farah near Izeh (Plates 14 and 15). The sacrifice of a humped ox, a chamois and three rams is accompanied by three musicians on harp, lyre and flute.

Ritual slaughter was also probably part of the daily 'routine' of an Elamite temple. At the consecration of the new Temple of Inshushinak at Susa, during which twenty measures of oil had been sprinkled on its portals, King Kutik-Inshushinak ordained a daily sacrifice, in the form of 'one wether in the high temple, one in the low temple'. We learn from account tablets that many centuries later the same high temple was still regularly supplied with sheep. But then a 'barley-fattened' sacrificial sheep was also the due to the foreign gods Nergal, Enki and Ninegal. Probably another would also be slaughtered in the temple before the throne and statue of the ruler, and the daily temple offerings were blessed not only by the ruler but also by his wife. Ritual slaughter for political motives is only mentioned in passing in Elam: on the departure for war, wethers were sacrificed in Susa before the huge statue of a lion, probably at the town gate.

There were however two special occasions in Elam which called for the ritual slaughter of animals. The most important seems to have been the festival of the 'mistress of the capital'. It is clear that since ancient times there had been an acropolis at Susa with a sacred precinct containing the temples of the various deities, dominated by the high temple of Inshushinak. The 'mistress of the capital' probably referred to Pinikir, and later perhaps to Kiririsha as well. The festival of the Great

Mother took place at the new moon towards the beginning of autumn, which was at that period also the beginning of the year. In the sacred grove of the goddess 'grown fattened wethers' were slain in a ritual manner that was known as the *gushun*. Since this festival was called a 'day of the flowing sacrifice', the flow of sacrificial blood was of prime importance. The accounts of the royal chamber make it evident that this festival of purification did not only take place in the sacred precinct, but also in the palaces of the king and queen. The necessary beasts of slaughter were selected from the royal flocks as early as the beginning of September, and their departure was duly 'booked' by the secretaries responsible in the proper official manner.

One particular day was also consecrated to the god Simut (Shimut). For his festival, known as a *tuga*, a bull was sacrificed; this took place annually, apparently in the middle of May. The animal was specially selected for the 'god of the Elamites', and was often brought from afar. On one occasion the Sumerian King Gungunum (who ruled from 1932 to 1906 B.C.) dedicated the bull for Simut's festival in person. In order to make a good impression on the Elamites, whose overlord he then was, he had the bull brought to Susa from the region of Zaban on the lower reaches of the River Zab. On its arrival, after several weeks on the hoof, it seems to have been cared for in the royal cowsheds until the sacrifice.

At all periods a priesthood was attached to the temple; in the capital the priests were certainly numerous, and had a large staff. At the head was the high priest. Even in Elamite inscriptions his title is only to be found in its Akkadian version, *pashishu rabu*; the ordinary priests always bore the Elamite title of *shaten*. Unquestionably, the high priest wielded great influence at court; he would often accompany the ruler on his military expeditions, and we hear of a later high priest, *Shutruru*, who received sacrificial cows in the places captured by Shutruk-nahhunte II and on that account erected stelae of the Elamite king .

The calendar also bears witness to the overwhelming influence of the priesthood upon the domestic life of the Elamite people. Right up to the middle of the second millenium B.C., November is called 'month of the ordering of the gods' fields' and December 'month of the field-furrow of the sowing'. The Elamites had first to put the temple fields in order before they were allowed to make a start on the sowing of their own fields. In the same way April was set aside for the barley harvest in the temple fields, and the fields of the lay Elamites had to wait their turn until May.

Control of the extensive temple estates and of the other goods which poured in for the gods was in the hands of the priests. For example, a tablet from Susa mentions that the foreign goddess *Anunitum*, acting through her priest, leased out a large field. The following early text is also significant: 'In town and country, for business in silver and gold, the sun-god and Lord Arad-Kubi are partners, just as his father before him. What his father did in business, he has done for the sun-god.' It goes without saying that it is not the god Nahhunte who was the partner of Arad-Kubi, but the high priest of his temple. Business consisted chiefly in lending capital – to women as well as to men – and also grain. Debts and interest usually had to be settled in the month of the Great Goddess, August.

The sources also mention Elamite oracle-priests. Their duty was probably to attempt to divine the decrees of the gods by inspecting the liver and other organs of the beasts they had sacrificed, or else by inducing, more or less artificially, a state of trance, much as the shamans did.

The Elamite priests seem to have been naked while exercising their religious functions. The principal evidence for this comes from pictures on seals and other small objects found above Susa *D*, i.e. from the end of the third millennium B.C. A bitumen carving dating from this period shows two naked

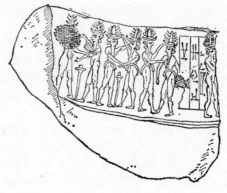

*Figure 27*

priests and a sacrificial lamb, surmounted by two snakes (Plate 22). The priests appear to be wearing wigs, which suggests that they were clean-shaven all over. A seal of the governor Eshpum of about 2300 B.C. portrays six male figures with horned crowns (Figure 27). They probably represent priests; two are naked, but the others seem to be wearing loin-cloths in the form of a snake. They stand in pairs, clasping each other's arms and crowns, as if they wanted to express their joy at the nomination of Eshpum as Governor.

In this connection a discovery dating from Elam's classical period is particularly revealing. It is a bronze model, dedicated by King Shilhak-Inshushinak in the second half of the twelfth century (Plate 23). It bears an inscription in Akkadian meaning 'sunrise'. In all probability the scene it represents was enacted regularly at sunrise. This model, unique of its kind, conveys vividly and clearly all the essential characteristics of Elamite worship.

The bronze introduces us to the sacred precinct, or *Siyankuk*, of Susa. Ziggurats rise on each side; a sacred grove grows in front of the smaller one, but its branches have almost completely worn away. In front of two pillars we can also see a sacrificial table; to it belong the huge earthen jar and the two stone basins or tubs. But all this is only the setting for the act

62

*Figure 28*

of worship itself. In the centre two naked male figures are half squatting, half kneeling; one of them, probably an assistant, is pouring water over the outspread hands of the other (Figure 28). This second figure is most likely the high priest. André Parrot was right when he wrote that: 'No liturgical event has ever been portrayed more exactly.'* To do justice to the scene, we must imagine that it is taking place, in stillness and dignity, in the morning twilight before the sun has appeared above the mountains of Anshan to the east of Susiana: the topmost leaves of the sacred grove are stirring in the cool and gentle breeze.

The gods of Elam were served not only by priests but also by priestesses. These, like their male colleagues, occupied themselves in administration. According to one text, priestesses demanded – and received – large quantities of barley. According to another, a priestess undertook the sale of a house in collaboration with a businessman; she sealed the contract with her nail, and its imprint can still be discerned on the tablet today. One special group among the priestesses was formed by those women or maidens who had dedicated their lives to the Great Goddess. Our only information about them is unfortunately confined to arid administrative receipts from the early Babylonian period, and all they prove is that these servants

* *Sumer*, München, 1960, 332

of Pinikir or Kiririsha also possessed real estate and ran it at a profit.

One outstanding text should be mentioned at this point: the Akkadian brick inscription of a ruler of Susa who is otherwise nearly unknown; his name is *Tempt-ahar*, and he may have lived between 1500 and 1350 B.C. Tempt-ahar informs us that he has had a temple of baked brick built to the god Inshushinak, and that he has set up in it statues of himself and of his 'beloved handmaidens' (presumably his harem) and also portraits of two protective spirits, *Lamassu* and *Karibatu*.

The figures who guarded the interior of the temple may be conceived as sphinxes or gryphons or similar fabulous hybrids. Lamassu appears only once in Elamite inscriptions, by Shilhak-Inshushinak in the twelfth century. He tells us that there was a dilapidated statue of Lamassu made of unbaked clay in the Temple of Inshushinak at Susa, and that he had it repaired with terracotta. Assurbanipal, the conqueror of Susa, paid particular attention to the figures of Lamassu; he says in his report of the victory in 646 B.C.: 'I have had removed all the spirits without exception, including Lamassu the temple guardian.' For Lamassu was considered by the Assyrians, and by the Babylonians, to be a fearful she-devil, responsible for puerperal fever and infant mortality: 'You are an Elamite' is the half fearful, half defiant cry to Lamassu in a vow from Uruk in Mesopotamia. In Elam, however, Lamassu was obviously a provider of divine protection, who guarded the temple in happy conjunction with Karibatu, goddess of many blessings.

The brick text mentioned above also reports secret rites in the temple in connection with these very spirits. In it, King *Tempt-ahar*, relying on the dedication of the temple and of the effigies, openly counts on the favour and blessing of the god Inshushinak. Then the inscription continues: 'When night falls, four priestesses must enter the temple. So that they remove no gold [from the statues and hide it in] their loin-cloths, these shall be bound up tightly with thongs.' As the additions (in square brackets) show, this sentence is somewhat obscure. Should we infer from it that the protectresses of the temple wore only a loin-cloth, and that in spite of their sacred duty they were suspected of occasionally filching the gold overlay of the effigies?

The rest of the inscription is easier to understand. King Tempt-ahar adds: 'they (the four guardians) shall lie down under Lamassu and Karibatu. The governor, the chief of police, the high priest, the temple guards and the temple priest shall seal [the portals] on them. [The guardians] are to light lamps, and when morning dawns they are to commend the king to Lamassu and Karibatu, break open the seals, and take their leave.' Here we are obviously being told of an 'incubation', which would be undertaken every night with the elaborate assistance of persons of importance. We can only guess at the deeper meaning of this cult act. It may be that the four protectresses were at the service of the two demi-gods during the night, and that as a reward they were permitted to implore their blessing on the king. It seems strange that such careful precautions accompanied the incarceration of the maidens and the sealing of the temple, when they were obviously allowed to leave at dawn without any formalities whatever.

This text throws a ray of light on a secret ritual, but at the same time – typical of the Elamites, one is tempted to say – it obscures it. At least it was fortunate that Tempt-ahar had the bricks inscribed in Akkadian; had they been written in Elamite, they would still remain shrouded in mystery.

Finally, let us look at the Elamite attitude to the hereafter. Did they believe at all in a life after death?

Most of the evidence is to be found in their graves. Almost invariably a clay jar was placed in them as an offering. When an ordinary Elamite died, he was simply placed unshrouded under the floor of his hut; but, however poor, a clay pot was always buried at his feet. The wealthy, too, were provided with such vessels, whether they were interred in clay coffins or in beautifully constructed brick vaults. There were also channels along which water could be poured into the graves: the Elamites held the view that drink as well as food was necessary after death.

Assurbanipal boasts that he laid waste the burial vaults of the Elamite kings, exposed them to the light of day, dragged the bones of the corpses to Assyria, and – this is important – deprived their souls of rest by removing their burial offerings and libations. It is arguable that the Assyrian king was only imposing his own idea of the hereafter on Elam; but his report is confirmed by archaeological discoveries, which suggest that burial offerings and libations for the dead were the practice in Susa before Assurbanipal's appearance. Confirmation is also provided by domestic legal texts from the early Babylonian period; final codicils go to some considerable trouble to ensure that offerings would be brought to the testator regularly after his demise. The Elamites were convinced that such gifts eased the fate of the departed and would keep his soul from eternal unrest. An even clearer impression of the Elamite conception of the hereafter is to be found in seven tablets which were discovered in tombs at Susa. In spite of the fact that they are sometimes obscure or mutilated, these Akkadian texts are unusually revealing, as they are composed specifically for the dead and were put into the grave with them. They thus express the current opinion about death and the afterlife, if not the views of the dead themselves.

The first tablet is about an Elamite to whom life on earth has brought only misfortune. 'Up now, I will go, thou my god and lord,' it begins. 'God and lord' obviously means the guardian spirit who guided him through his life on earth. The Elamite intends to take his hand once he has traversed the grave, to appear before the great gods. 'I will hear my sentence and kiss your feet' : he will implore the support of his guardian spirit in the expected judgement. 'You let me wait upon you . . . May you at last, my god, take me to the realm of shadows. For my lot on earth was a slough of torture and despair, and yet on the sorrowful earth you allowed me but little water and verdure on the meadow of drought.'

From another tablet we have discovered the fact that Inshushinak also fulfilled the duties of a judge of the dead, and this theme is echoed in a third text : 'They remained standing, and those lie in an [underground] plot who once ruled the earth, who owned its hearths, who had nobody near them ... From now on only the god Inshushinak speaks his commands for ever in the grave.' The tablet concludes with the plea : 'May he refresh me with water, I who have entered the shadows.' The deceased referred to here was probably also one of those who once possessed earthly power and wealth, but who now, in the world of shadows, yearn for a draught of water.

The belief seems to have been held in Elam that a properly endowed grave could make an enormous difference to the departed. Another text affirms : 'The platters for his grave have been provided, and the stones for his shelter have been obtained – and so he may rejoice, who now goes to meet his fate ...'

Although so much still remains uncertain in these texts, we may detect in them the constant desire that the deity may welcome the departed, may fill his mouth with oil, may set meat and bread before him, and may provide him with wine or at least water. Behind the texts themselves there are unmistakable traces of the fear that accompanied every journey to the other world for everybody 'who has heard the summons and has sought out the grave to pass through it'.

All these pronouncements prove that a belief in a life after death was universal in Elam. The departed was, as we have seen, received by the two guiding goddesses Ishnikarab and Lagamal, and was led to Inshushinak, who pronounced his verdict in his capacity as the 'weigher of souls'. The Elamites do not appear to have awaited this pronouncement with much confidence, but the kingdom of shadows was not shrouded in the darkness of doubt and despair.

CHAPTER IV

# The First Thousand Years
# (c. 2500-1500 B.C.)

The history of Elam remains incomprehensible unless the geographical relationship between the plain and the mountains is constantly borne in mind. The bond between the fertile and well-watered meadows and farmland of Susiana and the high valleys and mountain-chains of Anshan in the north and east of the plain, rich in timber and in iron – this bond was the original basis of the independent character of Elam's history and civilization. When this vital link was broken in the seventh century B.C., and when the Medes and Persians took over the mountains of Elam, the country was doomed. It is probable that centuries of effort were needed to fuse the inhabitants of Susiana and the predominantly nomadic shepherds of the Anshan mountains into one Elamite people. Further, it appears that such a political unity was only achieved by rulers of strong character, and if none was forthcoming, the territories of Elam reverted to their original isolation.

For this reason, Elam was always structured as a *federal* state. In an attempt to unite the very diverse areas of the federation, the kings, being sovereign, strove to bind the minor princelings to themselves by the ties of blood relationship. The result was a body politic constructed on lines that were unusual, complicated, and indeed unparalleled elsewhere. The ruling houses most adept at this task all seem to have sprung from the high land and not from Susiana, although Susa itself early attained the status of capital.

We are almost entirely ignorant of the relationships between Elam and her neighbours in the mountains of Iran; there are, however, many indications that trade between them flourished and thus that relations were by and large peaceful. On the other hand, Elam's attitude to Mesopotamia is suggested by foreign and domestic accounts which are adequate even if occasionally inconsistent. The oldest information we have dates back to about 2680 B.C., when, according to the Sumerian king list, the half-legendary King Enmebaraggesi, of the first dynasty of Kish, 'carried off as booty the weapons of the land of Elam'. Even in the mists of this early period, the scholar can discern the characteristic mutual relationship between Elam and Mesopotamia – a continuing vendetta which only appears to have abated after equally lengthy commercial and cultural exchanges.

The countless campaigns against Elam that were undertaken by the Sumerians, the Babylonians and the Assyrians can on the whole be attributed to their efforts to gain for themselves the considerable resources that were only to be found in the mountains. We have already referred to them : timber, stone, iron and horses. The irruptions were also an attempt to deter the Elamites, with their ceaseless plundering greed, from attacking Mesopotamia. For these incursions were just as frequent as those of their enemies into Elamite territory. Thus the Sumerian king list informs us gloomily that later, probably between 2600 and 2550, the kingdom of Ur was 'struck with weapons and its kingship transferred to Awan . . .'

During the first millennium of Elamite history, between about 2500 and 1500 B.C., we are concerned chiefly with three ruling houses : the kings of Awan, the kings of Simashki, and the so-called 'Grand Regents' who probably originated in Simashki as well. So far the positions neither of Awan nor of

Simashki can be identified with certainty. Going on the immediate evidence of the sources, Awan may have lain in the environs of what is now Dizful, and Simashki in the north near modern Khurramabad.

According to these sources, there was very early a powerful Elamite kingdom of Awan, which appears to have managed to sustain a position of supremacy over Mesopotamia. However, in about 2550 B.C., a king of Kish succeeded in shaking off the yoke of Elam. Following a period of probable confusion in Elam, a new dynasty of twelve kings emerged. We only know the names of its founder *Peli* (the reading is not absolutely certain) and of his six successors (see the Chronological Tables). This dark period of Elamite history is illuminated by a single unexpected shaft of light, namely the fragment of an inscription from the temple of the goddess Kiririsha at Liyan on the island of Bushire, on the Persian Gulf; we have already referred to it in Chapter II (Figure 19).

We first feel firm ground beneath our feet when we come to the period of the great *Sargon of Akkad* in central Mesopotamia. His far-reaching policies enabled him not only to tame the restless mountain peoples in the Zagros, but also to stifle for a considerable period the Elamite threat to Mesopotamia. Hence the arrogant title he bestowed upon himself: 'King of Kish, conqueror of Elam and of Warahshi'. Warahshi is most likely the area of the mountains of Posht-e-Kuh and of the land around the upper Karkheh in the north-west of Susiana. Plainly, it maintained friendly relations with Elam, from motives of self-preservation. For every intended attack which the tyrants of Mesopotamia launched upon Elam had to pass through Warahshi.

Sargon of Akkad only undertook the perilous war against Elam when he had expanded and established his kingdom in the north, west and south; that is, only when his fifty-seven years of rule were drawing to a close – hardly before 2325 B.C. Later Babylonian 'omen texts' make it quite clear what a difficult undertaking this was. One of these omen texts tells us

*Map of Mesopotamia*

*Map of Elam*

that the goddess Ishtar has allowed a light to shine for Sargon 'who was moving into the land of Warahshi . . . when he pressed forward into the darkness.' The texts emphasize continually that the king has 'penetrated the gloom'. In this way they describe symbolically the troublesome advance that Sargon led through the inaccessible mountain forests of Luristan.

One of the two Sargon inscriptions that report on this expedition also contains the first certain dating of Elamite history: at that time, it says, 2325 B.C., King *Luh-ishshan,* eighth ruler of the house of Peli of Awan, was ruling in Elam. Sargon seems to have allowed him to remain on the throne of Elam as his vassal; the lord of Akkad had entered Susa victorious. From Susa, and also from Awan, he transferred huge quantities of plunder to Mesopotamia. Luh-ishshan seems to have died soon after. His successor as King of Awan was his son *Hishep-ratep.* This name could mean 'the nourishing re-nowned ones'; if my interpretation is correct, it refers to certain female godheads.

Scarcely had Sargon been succeeded in Akkad by his son *Rimush* (2316–2307) than King Hishep-ratep of Elam and King *Abalgamash* of Warahshi seized the opportunity to join forces in order to shake off the yoke of the dynasty of Sargon. But before King Rimush could think of quelling the rebellious mountain-dwellers, he first had to put down uprisings in the Mesopotamian hinterland. In 2312 B.C., following the conquest of Dêr (now Badra, Iraq), Rimush fought his way along the same difficult paths as once his father had done, into the mountains of Posht-e-Kuh up to the valley of the Karkheh. The allies were beaten and pursued down the valley into the plain of Susa. A second battle took place between Susa and Awan, on the river Kabnit, which may be identical with the Balarud, a tributary of the Diz.

The fate of King Hishep-ratep is not known; he seems to have come off lightly. His country on the other hand was cruelly ravaged by Rimush. The proof of this still survives in the form of vases discovered during excavations in Nippur and

Ur, which Rimush consecrated to his gods 'out of the plunder from Elam after he had subdued Elam and Warahshi'; and from the same haul he dedicated 'thirty pounds of gold, three thousand six hundred pounds of copper and six slaves of both sexes' to his god Enlil.

It is from this period of Akkadian domination of Elam by Rimush that we find the first indication of its federal constitution that we mentioned at the beginning. We encounter Zinuba, a brother of the Elamite King Hishep-ratep, who was his Viceroy at the same time, and also a 'governor of Susa' (i.e. of Susiana) called Epir-mupi, who was probably a son of Hishep-ratep's. This is the first example of the strange triarchy of Elam, which will frequently occupy us from now on and which is peculiar to Elam. The exact constitution of this 'Troika' and the accompanying right of heredity in the royal family will be more closely examined later. But it should be noted at this point that when the Viceroy Zinuba died, without ever achieving supremacy in the troika, his position as Viceroy was filled by Epir-mupi, Prince of Susiana. But nor, it seems, did *he* live long enough to take the further step to the throne, and his place was taken by a certain *Eshpum*. The actual king of Elam was at that time Helu of Awan, of whom nothing else is known.

Eshpum's seal bearing the frolicsome naked priests is already known to us from Figure 27. His accession may have been roughly simultaneous with *Manishtusu's* in Akkad. The latter had assassinated his brother Rimush in 2306 B.C., and then reigned till 2292. In honour of this new Mesopotamian ruler, Eshpum commissioned a stone statuette of Manishtusu in Susa and dedicated it to Narunte, the goddess of victory. And so Susiana began to adopt Akkadian and thus Semitic ways.

Manishtusu was even successful in his attempt to conquer Anshan and the coastal areas of Elam. One division of his army advanced along the land route to the Persian Gulf via Susa, and a second, under his personal command, crossed the Gulf in ships. One of Manishtusu's inscriptions states : 'With gifts and presents I led the king of Anshan and Sherihum to my lord the sun-god [Shamash].' The main objectives of this daring expedition were obviously the quarries and silver mines of the south Iranian mountains.

In the thirty-seven years under *Naram-Sin* (2291–2255), who succeeded Manishtusu as the last of the great Sargon dynasty, Elam finally becomes recorded in history. Naram-Sin expanded the Akkadian kingdom right down the Zagros from Eastern Anatolia to Mekrab in south-east Iran. And yet in his inscriptions we find no reports of a war against Elam. Meanwhile, in Elam itself, Helu of Awan had been succeeded by King *Hita*, with whom Naram-Sin formed a treaty in 2280 B.C., a treaty already mentioned in the last chapter in connection with Elamite religion. This is also the first important text for Elamite history; inscribed on both sides with two columns of writing, the clay tablet was found in Susa and is now in the Louvre. It is, unfortunately, in very bad condition.

The most remarkable point about this text is the fact that it is written in Elamite, whereas all other remains of the Sargonid period up to Naram-Sin are in Akkadian only. Unfortunately much of the inscription still defies elucidation, partly as a result of its damaged and fragmentary condition, and partly on account of our inadequate knowledge of the Elamite vocabulary.

G. C. Cameron was the first to put forward the theory that Naram-Sin's co-signatory in the treaty was King Hita, of whom nothing is known apart from his appearance in the Elamite king list. He may have hit upon the right solution, for one part of the inscription in bad condition appears to read: 'I, Hita, will try to ward off evil from the land of Akkad.' In any case, the treaty proves that the powerful Mesopotamian ruler attached some importance to the union with Elam; his intention was probably to hold the Gutians in check, in the mountains which bordered on Elam to the north, between what is now Hamadan and Lake Urmia (Lake Rezaiyeh). The text of the treaty was ceremonially preserved in the Temple of Inshushinak at Susa, and until recently remained buried in the rubble.

The treaty opens with the appeal that we have already quoted: 'Hear, Goddess Pinikir, and you good gods of heaven!' In the two first columns altogether thirty-seven deities are mentioned by name as guarantors of the treaty and all are invoked in the ratification: 'Even the kings pay homage to the gods.' It continues: 'A king is loyally committed to the (sun) god Nahhunte (written Nahiti); a king is the subject of Inshu-shinak.' This remarkable quotation has already attracted our attention as an expression of self-abasement before the powers of light and darkness, before the two lords of life on earth and life hereafter. The second column concludes with the sentence: 'I take the goddess Shiashum, the (moon-) god Napir, and the (victory-) goddess Narunte as my witnesses.'

In the third column the Elamite king vows: 'Naram-Sin's enemy is also my enemy, Naram-Sin's friend is also my friend.' And further: 'Hostages were taken; my subjects are to defend Naram-Sin's allies for the sake of the hostages.' This should probably be taken to mean that King Hita had to send hostages to Akkad, and so he is now demanding in this text that his subjects should defend the allied Akkadian armies against foreign attacks so that the Elamite hostages in Mesopotamia will not be endangered.

On the other side of the tablet are elaborate vows and maledictions, the majority of which are still obscure. The eleventh column might mean: 'May peace be preserved here. Even the kings pay homage to the gods... let discord cease. May the opponents (of the two allies) be destroyed. Let no more evil appear here. By our subjects may your (Naram-Sin's) enemy be conquered, your power reinforced, and all opposition be removed. Even kings pay homage to gods.' Finally, in column twelve, Elam's king affirms: 'As a supporter of Naram-Sin I have sacrificed to the god Inshushinak,' and he curses any who may steal the treaty from the temple.

At the ratification of the treaty, Naram-Sin came to Susa in person. For the occasion, his minister and oracle-priest dedicated a statue to the deity for the life of their lord. Even the Warahshi, allies of Elam, had to subject themselves to the King of Akkad. King Hupshumkipi was 'thrown into chains'. Nor did a happier fate await the other mountain rulers in the north-west of Elam : the Prince of Arman, now Hulwan, and in particular Satuni, King of the Lullubi in the modern Iraqi-Kurd region which lies between Sarpol in Iran and Sulai-manijja in Iraq. But when Naram-Sin attempted to overthrow Gutium, he overestimated his powers and was evidently sub-jugated by the Gutians towards the end of his reign.

This weakening of the kingdom of Akkad encouraged Hita's successor in Elam to shake off the tyranny of Naram-Sin's heir, *Shar-kali-sharri* (2254–2230), who throughout his reign had to join forces with the Gutians. Thus *Kutik-Inshushinak,* the last of the twelve kings of Awan, was able to reassert Elam's independence from Mesopotamia and to inaugurate a period of national prosperity. The resurgence of patriotism in Elam is reflected in Kutik-Inshushinak's practice – unique amongst the rulers of Elam – of employing the native linear script in his records on stone monuments (see Chapter II). He made his mark on posterity thanks to a large number of inscriptions both in Elamite and in Akkadian.

The first post he occupied seems to have been that of 'Governor of Susiana', when Naram-Sin was still supreme. His father Shinpi-hish-huk may have been a younger brother of King Hita's and hence also Viceroy of Elam. Kutik-Inshu-shinak's real rise to power probably only began in 2250 B.C. under Shar-kali-sharri. It is clear from four inscriptions that he had now adopted the titles 'Governor of Susiana', 'Viceroy of the land of Elam'. And so, although Kutik-Inshushinak was not actually king at the time, he *was* striving to establish and strengthen his power by extensive military operations.

The first of his military expeditions took him right into Mesopotamian territory, to the upper Diyala, where the terri-tories of Kimash and Khurti had revolted against Shar-kali-sharri. It is conceivable that the King of Akkad had sought the help of his Elamite vassals in quelling this uprising. However, this did not satisfy Kutik-Inshushinak; he also overcame *Hupsana* (*Hupshen*), now known to us as Deh-e nou, on the Loreh, a tributary of the river Diz (Plate 3). An Akkadian inscription on a limestone statue, probably plundered by Kutik-Inshushinak in Mesopotamia, gives us an account of just this military success by the 'Viceroy of Elam'. In it, over seventy places are listed as having been 'thrown under his feet at one blow' – a claim that is certainly exaggerated, for whereas one of these places, Gutu, indicates the land of Gutium far in the north, another, Huhnur, probably lies near Basht in the Bakht-yari mountains to the east of Susa. The inscription concludes with the arrogant assertion that even the King of Simashki has come of his own free will and has 'seized the feet' of Kutik-Inshushinak, i.e. has entreated his protection and forgiveness. This last sentence now has a grim and prophetic touch because supremacy over the land of Elam devolved after Kutik-Inshushinak's death on the house of Simashki.

The next to accede to the throne of Elam was, of course, Kutik-Inshushinak himself; in 2240 he became King of Elam, the heir to Hita. In two of his Akkadian inscriptions he describes himself as 'Mighty king of Awan', and in Elamite linear inscriptions as 'King of the land, a chosen one, a victor'. He boasts on one stele that god Inshushinak 'has looked merci-fully on him and given him the four quarters of the earth'. The last remaining traces of vassaldom to Akkad and to her king Shar-kali-sharri are now erased by claims to domination in the Mesopotamian-Iranian area.

Kutik-Inshushinak dedicated a great new temple in Susa to his 'Lord Inshushinak', offering the many and varied sacri-ficial gifts that have been described in Chapter III. One stone monument from the temple depicts the king kneeling in order to present the deity with a bolt fashioned of bronze and cedar-wood; his wife is standing behind him with both hands raised (Plate 28). Further, the construction of a canal at Sidari is dedicated to him; in the relevant inscription we are informed that he has 'pronounced a just judgement in his city'. The king was confident that he was protected and supported by his gods. If my interpretation of the difficult Elamite in the native linear script is correct, he affirms with great pathos that his reward for the cult ceremonies and sacrifices he has made to the gods has been fame: 'The deities made me victorious, they gave me the land.'

The longest of his inscriptions in Elamite linear script is here reproduced in sketch form (Figure 29). It appears on a stone next to a carved snake, and in translation reads more or less as follows:

> I am Kutik-Inshushinak, king of the land, a chosen one. I consecrate this snake as a statue. May the land belong to god Inshushinak as a deity! May the sacrificing priest effect the grace of the goddesses throughout the land! I will bring thanks for it to the deity. This inscription was consecrated and set up to the god of the dedication. The inscription was blessed by divine grace. I possess this land. It was preserved for me as one of the deity's elect!

When we remember that the comparatively large number of Kutik-Inshushinak's surviving inscriptions are only a fraction of those which he originally commissioned, we can form a picture from the former of a ruler of influence and character, infused with strong nationalist feelings. In Kutik-Inshushinak, Elam beheld the personification of a political independence which had for so long been suppressed.

This period of Kutik-Inshushinak's supremacy was immediately succeeded in 2220 B.C. by the downfall of his house, the dynasty of Awan. And, as we have said, the Elamite linear script disappeared along with him and his nationalist pride. It seems likely that, like Akkad her neighbour, once her overlord but now no longer so powerful, Elam fell victim to the confusion engendered by the revolts of the Gutians.

In a king list discovered in Susa, we find recorded after the

*Figure 29*

twelve kings of Awan an equally long succession of kings of Simashki. According to the list, it seems most probable that the new dynasty had its origins in the mountains of Luristan in the north of Susiana, and its seat at Khurramabad. The fact that the new ruling house of Elam was also composed of exactly twelve kings leads to the suspicion that the list was artificially curtailed. And so we shall confine ourselves hereafter to a consideration of those kings of Simashki with impeccable historical references – and these are indeed few. For the obscurity that overshadows the end of the kingdom of Awan is not dispelled with the rise of the kingdom of Simashki.

The supremacy of the Gutians petered out miserably under their King Tirigan in 2120 B.C.; throughout its duration – a whole century – Elam only appears in the inscriptions of the Sumerian ruler Gudea of Lagash. The latter boasts on one of his statues that he conquered 'with weapons the town of Anshan in Elam', and asserts on a cylinder : 'Elamites came from Elam, Susians from Susa' – that is, came to help him in the reconstruction of a temple. On this evidence it would seem that Elam lay under the influence of the south-Mesopotamian princes of Lagash while the Gutians were supreme in northern Babylonia. The same impression of Elamite impotence arises when the Sumerian dynasty of Ur III seized power in south Mesopotamia. The dynasty was inaugurated in 2114 B.C. by King Urnammu and established a *pax Sumerica*, a 'Sumerian peace', welcome indeed to the Elamites but unfavourable to the expression of Elamite patriotism.

The Sumerian supremacy was most evident in Elam under the lengthy rule of *Shulgi* (2095–2048). It is true that Shulgi was forced to undertake several military expeditions against the restless mountain Elamites in Anshan; however, Susiana had been completely subjected to him since his victory over it in 2078 B.C., the twenty-eighth year of his rule, and had even been controlled for a considerable period by foreign governors. Shulgi was plainly successful in persuading the native priests to join his side, for he, the 'mighty king of Ur, Sumeria and Akkad', erected a temple in Susa to 'his king, the god Inshushinak', and endowed it generously with religious offerings. These have been preserved for posterity because subsequent Elamite rulers incorporated them in the foundations when reconstructing the temple.

Towards the end of his forty-eight years of rule, Shulgi hit upon a new method of protecting the kingdom of Ur, a method which was enforced throughout three generations of princes of the Ur III dynasty but which was in the end responsible for the downfall of the house in which it had originated. The method involved the creation on Mesopotamian territory of an Elamite 'foreign legion', whose principal duty was to reinforce the Sumerian garrisons but which was also to fend off the restless mountain peoples around the Zagros. These 'legionaries' were drawn, according to administrative texts, from Susa, from the eastern mountains of Anshan, and from Simashki. Probably Elamite prisoners-of-war were also enrolled. These Elamites worked in groups of five to twenty-five men, drawing a daily ration of barley bread and ale. The Elamite 'legion' was under the control of a high dignitary in the service of the kings of Ur III; he bore the title of 'Grand Regent' (*sukkal-makh* in Sumerian), and may best be described as controlling border patrols against Elam and the eastern mountain races. The Grand Regent gradually acquired such power in this capacity that he was able to establish a personal dynasty in Lagash. His position made such an impression on his Elamite neighbours that the same Sumerian title, *sukkal-makh*, was bestowed on the dynasty that succeeded the house of Simashki.

Under the system of the Elamite 'foreign legion', serving under the kings of Ur III, Elam enjoyed unbroken peace for a considerable period. Shulgi's successor *Amar-Su'ena* (2047–2039) ruled Susiana as he did his own country, except that he undertook no architectural ventures in Susa. The first evidence of such ventures emerges under the reign of his successor *Shu-Sin* (2038–2030), when Susa's standing had deteriorated to that of a subject provincial town.

Almost two centuries had passed since the downfall of the house of Awan and the rise of the princes of Simashki, and not one inscription had so much as mentioned any of these Elamite kings, vassals of Sumeria. The first record of this type dates from 2033 B.C., and it is the name *Girnamme* that suddenly rises out of the mist that had for so long shrouded the history of Elam. The name is also to be found in the Susa king list, in which it is bestowed on the first of the 'twelve' kings of Simashki; however this must be incorrect. We hear of Girnamme in an insignificant Sumerian tablet: an ambassador from King Girnamme has arrived in the court of *Shu-Sin* and there received a grant of some wethers for his keep.

As his great-grandfather Shulgi had done before him, so Shu-Sin married one of his daughters to the 'Prince of Anshan'. It is not clear from the texts whether this refers to King Girnamme of Simashi or only to one of his Elamite vassals in the eastern mountains. In the second year of Shu-Sin's rule, 2037 B.C., a deputy from this prince of Anshan had arrived in the Sumerian capital of Ur. It was in his company, loaded with provisions, that the princess embarked upon the long journey into the Bakhtyari mountains: the accounts at the court of Ur record many jars of oil, butter, cream, soured milk, ale, and so forth as being 'in tare'. Surely the king's daughter never dreamt that her brother *Ibbi-Sin* would take the same route thirty years later, no longer as ruler of Ur and lord of Elam, but as a prisoner of the King of Elam.

In 2029 Ibbi-Sin had succeeded his father in Ur, but only a few years later, King *Lurak-luhhan* of Simashki, successor to Girnamme, had launched an attack on Susiana from the mountains, and had in one swoop freed the towns of Awan (?Dizful), Adamdun (?Shushtar) and Susa. The young Sumerian king took up the challenge. After careful religious preparation, he led a lightning attack on Elam, regaining the towns he had lost. Lurak-luhhan of Simashki was taken captive and dragged to Ur in triumph. However, five years later, in 2017 B.C., Ibbi-Sin had once again to march against the refractory Elamites;

83

the fourteenth year of his reign is characterized thus : 'Year in which Ibbi-Sin marched with a huge army to Huhnur, the key of the land of Elam, and brought it to obedience.'

This expedition of 2017 was the last attempt the expiring kingdom of Ur III made to keep Susiana in subjection. Ibbi-Sin's power had been undermined by famine, by the attacking west-Semitic Amorites, and by the downfall of his ally *Ishbi-erra* on the central Euphrates; this enabled the new king of Simashki, probably *Hutran-tempt*, to overrun the southern part of Mesopotamia in a single invasion in 2006. Ibbi-Sin, after desperate resistance, had to 'arise from his palace' in Ur 'and go into the land of Elam, from the mountains of Sabum, the "breast" of the range, to the end of Anshan' (that would be along the Kabir-Kuh, right across Susiana, and then on to the Izeh/Isfahan route), as we are told in a Sumerian dirge; 'like a bird that has flown from its nest, like a stranger who [returns no more] to his home.'

At this period, Ur had been reduced by the Elamite troops to 'hills of ruin and places of desolation'. The King of Simashki, who may have been helped in Sumeria by the Elamite 'foreign legion', had garrisoned the acropolis at Ur, and had dragged the statues of the Sumerian moon-god Nanna and of other deities to Anshan, along with the captive Ibbi-Sin the last King of Ur III, who died there in exile. These revolutionary events made a deep impression in Mesopotamia; their reverberations were still felt long after in laments and predictions.

It was of course a long time before Elam's complete independence from Mesopotamia was assured under the kings of Simashki. The birthright of Ur III was soon usurped by the able Princes Ishbi-erra of Isin and Naplanum of Larsa, who must have been concerned to regain Susiana at least. And so it is not surprising that as early as 1993, thirteen years after the downfall of Ur, Ishbi-erra 'smote Elam with arms.' Significantly, this was the same year in which he betrothed his daughter to *Humban-shimiti*, probably the son of Hutran-tempt, who was at that time 'Regent' (*sukkal* in Sumerian) of Susiana.

So the heirs of the kingdom of Ur III persisted in the traditional Mesopotamian policy towards Elam, a policy that alternated between military coercion and diplomatic marriages. Ishbi-erra was not able to expel the Elamite settlers from Ur until 1985, twenty-one years after Hutran-tempt had captured it; and the restitution of the stolen moon-god Nanna was only achieved by his son and heir *Shu-ilishu* (1984–1975). This probably took place under the rule of Hutran-tempt's brother and successor *Kindattu*, between 1990 and 1970.

The latter, a shadowy figure, was succeeded in Elam as King of Simashki by his nephew, an outstanding ruler who appears in the king list as Indattu I; his full name was *Indattu-Inshushinak*, son of Pepi and 'sister-son' (*ruhu-shak* in Elamite) of Hutran-tempt. He had already been governor of Susiana and Viceroy of Elam, and was at that period encouraging a policy of considerable reconstruction in Susa: he saw to it that the ruined fortifications were repaired, that a new city wall was erected, and that the temple of Inshushinak was rebuilt of brick. It was to this shrine that he dedicated a limestone basin, inscribed in Akkadian; it still survives.

When Indattu-Inshushinak acceded to the throne in 1970 B.C., he installed his son *Tan-ruhurater* as Governor of Susa; this was a long-established tradition that we shall examine more closely later. A marriage was also arranged between him and Mekubi, daughter of Prince Bilalama of Eshnunna in Babylonia. This is the first occasion when Indattu-Inshushinak adopts the title of 'King of Simashki and Elam'. We may deduce from this that Elam, throughout the early period, comprised only Susiana and the eastern mountains of Anshan. The northern seat at Simashki may well first have been added to the kingdom by the kings of Simashki.

Indattu-Inshushinak was followed in 1945 B.C. by his son Tan-ruhurater, whose marriage to the Babylonian Mekubi resulted in the birth of a son who was to succeed his father in 1925 as *Indattu II*; while he was still governor in Susa under his royal father Tan-ruhurater, he also inspired a burst of

*Figure 30*

architectural activity. According to the inscriptions, he did not repair the old walls, cemented with bitumen, that surrounded the temple grounds, but had them replaced by new brick ones.

There is only one record discovered in Susa that dates from the actual rule of Indattu II, a delightful seal impression (Figure 30). Indattu is seated to the left, on a simple throne, clad in turban and costly garments. With his right hand he is presenting a curved staff to a figure who is identified by the Akkadian superscription as his chancellor (*teppir* in Elamite) *Kuk-Simut*. The third figure, a goddess in a tucked robe, is a joyful witness of the nomination of the chancellor. The staff-like object is clearly a symbol of ministerial dignity.

Those who held office as *teppir* were, as we shall see in the next chapter, also judges. Besides these duties, the chancellor of Elam was also responsible for the 'tablet-house' or scribes' school in which future high officials were taught the refinements of cuneiform script. Indeed, a tablet, written by Kuk-Simut himself, still survives, in which he reproaches the head of the school, Turukuzu, with unnecessary severity towards the budding secretaries. It reads thus: 'Chancellor Kuk-Simut to Turukuzu: Why do you torment the pupil scribes? My instructions are not to harass them.' The Akkadian tablet, in which only the term 'pupil scribes' (*puhu-teppi*) is in Elamite, is an historical rarity and affords us a glimpse into the tablet house at Susa four thousand years ago, disclosing that severe schoolmasters vented their wrath on their pupils even then. But the pupils no doubt included a ministerial offspring, whose father presented himself to the chancellor with a request for less rigorous discipline in the school.

The later Elamite kings, who inherited and bequeathed reliable family archives, allow the line of the kings of Simashki to fade out without comment on the death of Indattu II. It appears that only the mountains of Luristan were at this stage independent in Elam. In Figure 30, Indattu only describes himself as 'governor' (*ensi* in Sumerian) of Susiana. And Gungunum, the fifth ruler of Larsa in Sumeria, boasted of two victories over Anshan in 1930 and 1928. The details of the downfall of the kingdom of Simashki are no more discoverable than in the case of the collapse of Awan. Only the names of the last two kings of Simashki are extant: *Indattu-napir* and *Indattu-tempt*. While the great *Hammurabi* (really Khammurapi) of Babylon was involved in desperate struggles for power in order to establish his government in Mesopotamia, Elam vegetated peacefully, far from the turmoil of world politics.

The position of King of Simashki was superseded in about 1890 by a new and powerful dynasty. Its founder, a certain *Epart*, was apparently an upstart who, far from inheriting control of Elam, had seized it by force; sources are conspicuously uncommunicative about his origins. The internal records of the new ruling house of the Eparti are contained almost exclusively in about nine hundred clay tablets written in Akkadian; the majority of them are legal in character, the remainder administrative, but almost all of them are from Susa; a dozen or so appear to come from Huhnur. Only one of the Eparti is mentioned in an Elamite text and so far only one archaeological find has been unearthed from the three centuries of the grand regency, between about 1800 and 1500 B.C. And yet, however limited these texts may seem, they do throw light on two important functions: the constitution and the law. Chapter V will be devoted to the latter, but we shall deal with the former now.

An acquaintance with the Elamite constitution is indispensable to an understanding of her history, and its principles are apparent from the legal tablets just referred to. However, its peculiarities only emerge after a close examination of the formal oaths that are contained in the source material. It then becomes clear to the practised eye that the startling distribution of supreme power reflected in these tablets was by no means confined to the time of the Eparti. Quite the contrary: it was already in existence under the Kings of Awan and Simashki and remained in force through all later periods until the downfall of the kingdom in 640 B.C. The following outline of the Elamite constitution can therefore be said to apply throughout its history.

From the beginning we find that the federation of Elam was controlled by a *sovereign*, with power over a whole host of vassal-princes. During Elam's independence this sovereign was given the title of 'king' (*zunkir* in Elamite) to which 'of Anshan and Susa' was generally added. In the early Babylonian period, the title appears as a rule in Sumerian as *sukkal-makh*, meaning 'Grand Regent'. Apart from the king, Elam (and indeed her ally Warahshi) was ruled by a *Viceroy*. According to federal law he was the younger brother of the king and also his successor; and thus the Elamite constitution was based on the right of brothers, or fratriarchy: heirs to the throne are not the ruler's sons but his brothers. The viceroys hardly left a single inscription, and so their Elamite title remains unknown. During the period of the 'Grand Regents' they are described in the legal texts, half Sumerian, half Akkadian, as 'Regent of Elam and Simashki'. The Viceroys probably lived at the original seat of the dynasty, the cradle of their power, but certainly not at Susa. At first this seat was Awan; under the Grand Regents it was Simashki; and later still it probably moved to Anshan, south-east of Susiana.

Third place in the constitution was reserved for the ruler of Susiana or the 'Prince of Susa'. His Sumerian title was *sukkal*, 'regent', in Akkadian *sharrum*, 'king' (of Susa); in Elamite his office was described as 'land-bailiff' or 'governor' (*hal-menik*).

In theory, the Prince of Susiana was the eldest son of the sovereign.

The father, his nearest brother and his eldest son: these three men governed Elam. This triarchy, first recognized by G. G. Cameron, developed on the one hand from the early Elamite right of heredity, on the other from the laxity of the union between the federal states. The supreme power in the land was all the more active for being threefold, for the Viceroy – and heir to the throne – far from wasting his time in the dynastic seat, seems to have undertaken regular tours through the individual states, a practice that much enhanced their unity. Father and son, on the other hand, both remained in Susa, the capital. One cannot but wonder whether the close proximity of father and son led to dangerous tensions. Were there not kings in Elam who slew their sons?

Apparently not. Indeed, the ruler seems to have allowed his son considerable licence in Susiana; for example, decrees made by the father as sovereign only became legally valid in Susiana when ratified by his son as Prince of Susa. And then the inscriptions confirm that father and son would co-operate as friends over matters of construction in the capital. At times of drought and famine, legal tablets show a particularly striking family loyalty in Elam, not only in the ruling house itself, but among the ordinary people. Finally, it should not be forgotten that the son, as Prince of Susa, was no more than a provisional heir to the throne, for the king's brothers were next in line. This consideration may well have been decisive in eliminating the tension between father and son that would otherwise have been likely even in so family-minded a country as Elam.

How exactly did the right of inheritance work between the three rulers? The constitution demanded that the death of the king should result in the accession of his younger brother, the Viceroy. The brother's right of inheritance was the practice among the common people in Elam since early times; the prior claims of mother and brother were marvellously interwoven. However, during the second millennium, the fraternal rights of inheritance were slowly rejected by the common people in favour of the claims of the son, which eventually gained total acceptance. But not in the ruling house : there the brother's right of inheritance remained in force until the downfall of the kingdom, although towards the end it was often flagrantly infringed.

After the accession of the Viceroy to the throne, it was now not the Prince of Susa, the eldest son of the late sovereign, who became Viceroy, but the younger brother of the new sovereign and previous Viceroy. The Prince of Susa thus remained in office under his two uncles. In the period between 1850 and 1500 there were no fewer than five occasions on which a Prince of Susa continued in office under two consecutive Grand Regents; this indicates the close-knit connections between different members of the ruling house. When the sovereign died, his son would quite naturally have felt impelled to make a bid for the succession, and surely such dissensions cannot have been unknown within the bosom of the royal family. But there is no hint of them in the sources, and the general impression remains that there were no serious infringements of the tradition of the uncle's right of accession by his nephew.

In return, the late Viceroy, newly elevated to the position of sovereign, resisted any temptation to oust his nephew from his post as Prince of Susa and to install his own son in his place. It is true that on three occasions an Eparti ruled as Grand Regent together with two consecutive Princes of Susa, and once with three, but it would be incorrect to infer from this that the Grand Regent forcibly substituted one prince for another. It is more likely that the position became vacant through the prince's death, for it is clear that the ruling houses of Elam were bedevilled by an uncommonly high mortality rate.

It was this factor above all others that prevented a strict enforcement of the laws of inheritance when the throne became vacant. It only happened once that three brothers succeeded each other as sovereign in Elam, and that not until the seventh century B.C. Generally only two brothers are to be found in one generation, and so quite commonly a cousin had to stand deputy for the missing brother. Only when the generation of the brothers and cousins had been exhausted could the Prince of Susa accede to the Vice-regency, and only then could the current sovereign elect his own son as Prince of Susa. But, as we shall see, all too often he had no sons, and then the only solution was to have recourse to his nephew.

The high mortality rate in the ruling houses of Elam was very probably the result of incest, a practice that was the outcome of two further peculiarities of the inheritance : the practice of levirate and marriage between siblings. On the death of the sovereign, his brother would succeed him and would marry his widow; she again was customarily the sister of both of them. Marriage between siblings had been postulated for some time and was indirectly confirmed by the texts; the first direct reference emerged when the word for 'sister' (*shutu*) was established, explaining an awkward passage in an inscription of Prince Hanne dating from about 710 B.C., in which he describes the Princess Huhin as his 'beloved sister-spouse'. The results of such genetically harmful relationships were inevitable, and led to a permanent disruption of the laws of inheritance; in practice the father was often succeeded by his son, simply because the deceased ruler was survived neither by his brothers nor by his cousins, or because he never had any brothers.

The Elamite constitution is characterized by intermarriage, levirate and triarchy; as such it is without parallel in world history.

As regards the third ruling house within the thousand years between 2500 and 1500, I shall confine myself to isolating the most important events of Elamite history.

The founder of the dynasty was Epart – referred to above. The texts reveal very few facts about him, the most important thing being the title he bestowed upon himself : 'King of

Anshan and Susa', which was at that time a novelty and which seemed to the Elamites like a call to arms. Geographically speaking, this title included the whole of Elam; constitutionally speaking, it asserted the independence of the country as a kingdom.

Epart's rise to power, dating from 1890 B.C., seems to have been gradual and not without difficulties. He appears to have died relatively soon after his accession. On every tablet that survives from his reign, emphasis is given to his royal title: he never refers to himself as 'Governor' or even 'Grand Regent'. Still more significant is the only tablet surviving from the first year of his reign; here, in the Sumerian date formula 'year in which Epart became king', his name is preceded by the sign for a deity. This is the first and only time that an Elamite ruler was deified, although this practice was common in Sumeria and not unknown in Babylonia. The inconspicuous sign *dingir* (Sumerian for 'deity') on the inconspicuous tablet that records the receipt of beasts of sacrifice from the royal sheep-folds at Susa suggests to us that the arrival of Epart was an unusually impressive event; this is confirmed by an omen about Epart that survived as far away as Babylonia. However, this deification was abandoned almost as soon as it was adopted: while Elam's kings considered themselves as the tools and servants of the gods, and hence as the recipients of their special protection, they never saw themselves as equals.

In accordance with tradition, Epart nominated his son *Silhaha* as Prince of Susa. A cylinder (Figure 31) survives from this period which Silhaha's chancellor *Kuk-tanra* dedicated to the sovereign, Epart. Kuk-tanra, on the left, is being conducted to the seated ruler by a goddess in a tucked robe, presumably in order to have his appointment as chancellor to Silhaha confirmed. Even in this scene, we sense something of the peculiar power that Epart exercised over his contemporaries, for on this seal he appears in an almost god-like capacity. And yet Silhaha, destined to a comparatively long reign after Epart's death, has now so obscured his father's fame that it is

*Figure 31*

he and not Epart whom history accepts as founder of the dynasty.

A third figure stands out from the early years of the dynasty: Epart's daughter. Her name is unknown, but as 'Silhaha's sister' she achieved the position of ancestral mother to the dynasty. The later Eparti were not considered true heirs to the throne unless they could trace their descent from Silhaha's sister, the 'gracious mother' (*amma hashuk*). Plainly, a legitimate claim to the throne, inherited from the 'distaff side' and coexistent with the fraternal right of accession, was accepted in Early Elam as the legacy of ancient matriarchal assumptions.

On his accession, Silhaha described himself as 'Grand Regent, father-king of Anshan and Susa'. This may sound pompous, but it is the first time that the title of 'Grand Regent' is to be found in Elam, and indicates a certain independence towards Mesopotamia. At that time King *Apil-Sin* (1830–1812) was probably reigning in Babylon. It is clear that Silhaha was unable to maintain completely the independence that his father had won from King *Sabium* of Babylon; subsequent rulers abandon the formality of the arrogant title 'King of Anshan and Susa', and it was not until the patriotic revival of Elam's 'classical' period in the twelfth to thirteenth centuries that the title was adopted once more. From *Untash-napirisha* on (about 1275) it became the accepted royal title.

When Silhaha came to the throne, he installed his 'sister's son' *Attahushu* as Regent of Susa – presumably because he himself had no sons. However, the decisive factor in his election was the fact that Attahushu was the eldest son of the 'gracious mother', Silhaha's sister. This nephew at once embarked on a policy of extensive innovation in Susa. As his grandfather Epart and uncle Silhaha had done before him, he added to the Temple of Inshushinak, and christened himself his 'beloved servant'. It was he who completed the temple of the moon-god, already begun under the joint efforts of Epart and Silhaha. One of Attahushu's Akkadian inscriptions states that he, as 'shepherd of the people of Susa', for the safety of their life, dedicated a temple to the 'great mistress Ninegal' (Pinikir). He also commemorated in a shrine the Elamite goddess of victory, Narunte, and Anunitum, her Akkadian counterpart.

To the west of Susa, on the other side of the Ulai, Attahushu built a fortified palace, linking it to the capital by a bridge. One last testimony to his many and varied activities as Prince of Susa is to be found in the 'stele of righteousness' that he erected in the market-place at Susa to act as an official price index. Its inscription contains an appeal to the sun-god Nahhunte to encourage universally fair prices. Attahushu clearly established a precedent, for the 'great table' is mentioned in later texts in connection with the grain trade; it probably had the top prices for corn inscribed upon it.

It appears that Attahushu died before his uncle; for when Silhaha died, it was Attahushu's younger brother *Sirktuh I* who acceded to the throne. He in his turn nominated *his* younger brother *Simut-wartash* as Viceroy. They both styled themselves Silhaha's nephews, as Attahushu had done.

To begin with, Sirktuh I ruled without a Prince of Susa, and we may deduce from this that he had no son. His final solution to the problem was an astonishing one, Elamite in its ingenuity. He chose that famous sister of Silhaha, the 'gracious mother', as Princess of Susa: in other words, his own mother. This is the only time that we hear of an Elamite queen ruling officially, and it was not until her death that the post was transferred to Sirktuh's nephew *Siwe-palar-huhpak*.

Under the triarchy of Sirktuh I (Grand Regent), his brother Simut-wartash (Viceroy) and his nephew Siwe-palar-huhpak (Prince of Susa), we are already in the period of the rise of the first dynasty of Babylon under King Hammurabi (1792–1750). The scanty evidence to be found in the texts indicates that Sirktuh was attempting to oppose the Babylonian tyranny by a policy of aggression. One tablet (written in 1790 B.C. but not discovered till 1957 at Shusharra, near modern Rania, in the Kurd area of Iraq) proves that Sirktuh was then still independent, for he is still given the royal title. Sources from Mari reveal that the King of Elam had allied himself to the King of Eshnunna in Babylonia, not far from Baghdad; Sirktuh himself led a summons to arms to Eshnunna. The allied troops besieged the town of Razama, but Hammurabi forced them to raise the siege. It may be that Sirktuh himself fell on this occasion, for a tablet from Mari states that letters were captured during the battle, according to which the 'Regent of Susa and Elam' had been killed.

In 1770 B.C., Sirktuh was succeeded by his younger brother Simut-wartash, the Viceroy; the position he vacated was filled by his nephew Siwe-palar-huhpak, who was in his turn replaced as Prince of Susa by another nephew, *Kuduzulush* (I). But Simut-wartash's reign was brief, and on his death in 1768 his nephew Siwe-palar-huhpak came to the throne as ordained by constitutional law. Meanwhile in the rest of the Near East, the delicate balance of power between a dozen states was tending increasingly to favour Babylon under Hammurabi. Faced with his rise to power, King *Zimrilim* of Mari joined Hammurabi's opponents, and a coalition of totally incongruous allies was formed against him, in which Siwe-palar-huhpak may have played an important part. The King of Eshnunna was already an old-established Elamite ally; he was now joined by the Queen of Nawar in the Iranian-Kurdian mountains of Gutium (she allegedly contributed ten thousand men); also the King of Malgium (on the Tigris, to the south of its junction with the Diyala); and the King of the Subarians of Assur.

However, as a result of a number of large-scale military operations, Hammurabi retained the upper hand over all his opponents, and his first victory, a decisive one as far as Elam was concerned, was gained in 1764, before Zimrilim of Mari had joined the allies. Swelling with pride – justifiably – Hammurabi reports that he 'reduced the army of Elam, which had irrupted at the Warahshi border, to submission, along with the Subarians, the Gutians, Eshnunna and Malgium, who had rallied with their hosts.' At which point, Elam opted out of Mesopotamian political life.

It is true that this submission is belied by an inscription of Siwe-palar-huhpak's – incidentally the only Elamite text from the millennium between 2250 and 1280 B.C. – in which the Grand Regent describes himself simply as 'Governor of Elam'. The royal title has vanished, and he probably avoided the use of the phrase 'Grand Regent' on purpose, inspired by sentiments of national pride. This Elamite tablet is also important because idioms contained in it are not used again for six hundred years, and then – significantly – without linguistic variation. The historian is constantly staggered by the conservative habits of the Elamites; some scholars would prefer to question the authenticity of this inscription, but I cannot subscribe to their views. I reproduce it here in translation, as accurately as the lacunae and linguistic problems permit, on account of its enormous social and historical value. It reads: 'O God Inshushinak, thou lord of the capital (Susa). I am Siwe-palar-huhpak, increaser of the kingdom, governor of Elam, nephew of Sirktuh. For the benefit of my life, for the benefit of the lives of my gracious mother, of my older relatives and the younger, I have [ ... ]' The lacuna probably reads 'dedicated this temple'. It continues: 'O God Inshushinak, great lord! I, Siwe-palar-huhpak, have besought thee in sacrifice – grant my appeal! Through night and day I have truly committed the people of Anshan and Susa as a pledge for your mercy.' After a partly destroyed and indecipherable passage, the end of the text reads as follows: 'May fire consume the

*1. Susa today: the village of Shush with the tomb of Daniel*

*2. Excavation headquarters of the French Archaeological Mission in Susa*

*3. Deh-e nou, once Hupshen*

*4. The goddess Narunte*

5. *The heights at Kurangun*

*6. A Sassanid relief superimposed on an Elamite one, Naqsh-e Rostam*

*7. Relief of an Elamite pilgrimage, Kul-e Farah*

*8. Choga Zambil. View from the ziggurat into the Holy Precinct between the inmost and middle walls. In the background, the river Diz*

*9. Choga Zambil showing the ziggurat and its three encircling walls. North-west is at the top of the picture*

*10. Choga Zambil. On the left the south-west side of the ziggurat, on the right the south-east*

*11. Choga Zambil: part of the south-east face*

*12. A triple-arched niche on the round tower in front of the south-west entrance to the ziggurat of Choga Zambil*

*13. Choga Zambil: south-west entrance to the ziggurat*

*14. Relief of Hanne*
*Kul-e Farah (c. 710 B.C*

*15. Three musicians on the*
*relief of Prince Hanne in*
*the gorge of Kul-e Farah*
*near Izeh*

*16. The tepeh of Izeh (Malamir), once an Elamite stronghold*

*17. An Elamite relief in Qal'e-je Toll to the south of Izeh*

*18. Prince Hanne with his wife and son (a relief in the gorge of Shekaft-e Salman)*

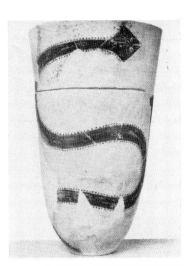

*19. Elamite head from Susa*

*20. A snake-vase from the level Susa A*

*21. Elam's treaty with King Naram-Sin of Akkad* (C. *2260* B.C.), *from the front*

22. *Naked priests on a bitumen relief from Susa B*

23. *A bronze model, 'Sunrise', dedicated by King Shilhak-Inshushinak* (c. *1150-1120* B.C.)

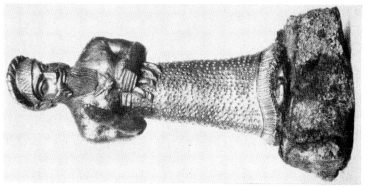

*24 and 25. Men bearing sacrifices from Susa: left, of silver, right, of gold*

*26. Goblet in the style of Susa A depicting a chamois, greyhounds, and birds*

27. *An Elamite king (on the left) before the sun-god Nah-hunte (a basalt stele 67 cm. high)*

28. *King Kutik-Inshushinak with his temple bolt; behind him, his wife* (C. 2250 B.C.)

29. *A bronze statue of Queen Napir-asu, wife of King Untash-napirisha* (c. *1250* B.C.)

30. *'Snake stele' of King Untash-napirisha*

*31. A bronze relief with Elamite warriors (eighth century B.C.?)*

*32. Relief of the penultimate king of Elam, Atta-hamiti-Inshushinak (653-648 B.C.)*

foes, may [their] allies hang on stakes! Burnt up, spurned, they shall lie in chains at my feet.'

If, as seems likely, this inscription was not written until the submission of 1764, the title 'Increaser of the kingdom' adopted by Siwe-palar-huhpak would seem out of place. However, it is conceivable that the Grand Regent attempted to compensate for his losses in Mesopotamia by victories in the high lands of Iran. This theory would be confirmed by a twelfth century report which makes it clear that, in the view of later Elamites, Siwe-palar-huhpak ranked among the great rulers of the kingdom. He was succeeded by his brother Kuduzulush I, most likely in 1745 B.C. After a period of solo rule, he nominated his nephew *Kuter-Nahhunte* as Prince of Susa.

It was this Kuter-Nahhunte I who rose to the Grand Regency in 1730; his first move was to nominate his brother *Lila-irtash* as Viceroy and his eldest son *Tempt-agun* as Prince of Susa. Kuter-Nahhunte I left his mark not only on the kings of Elam but also on later Assyrian rulers. Under Hammurabi's successor *Samsuiluna* (1750 – 1712), Babylonian power had lapsed so perceptibly that Kuter-Nahhunte was at last able to risk revenge for the submission forced on his uncle Siwe-palar-huhpak by Hammurabi. He may have seized his opportunity when *Abieshukh* took over the throne of Babylon from his father in 1711.

Over a thousand years later, Assurbanipal reported the terrible attack which the Elamites launched on Mesopotamia: 'Kuter-Nahhunte of the Elamites, careless of his oath to the great gods, and full of misplaced confidence in his own strength, laid hand on the shrines of Akkad, and levelled Akkad to the ground.' At the same time, Kuter-Nahhunte took the statue of *Nanaja*, the Mesopotamian goddess of victory and fertility, to Susa. The Assyrian king adds: 'Nanaia, who had been angry for one thousand, six hundred and thirty-five years' – this must be a scribal error, for the period between this report in 646 B.C. and Kuter-Nahhunte's attack was certainly no more than 1075 years – 'who had left us and established herself in Elam, a place unworthy of her, entrusted me with her return home.' And so Assurbanipal restored the goddess to Mesopotamia.

This victory over the Babylonians seemed splendid to that most resplendent of the kings of Elam, *Shilhak-Inshushinak* (*c.* 1150–1120). He informs us on a stele that he wishes to 'prove the honour of Kuter-Nahhunte and his [son and prince of Susa] Tempt-agun' because they had overcome thirty towns in Mesopotamia. Kuter-Nahhunte had taken possession of the land of Akkad as 'possessor and master', condemning the domestic rulers to oblivion. Thus he filled the Babylonians once more with 'fear and awe of the Elamite people'. The memory of this great victory may have inspired King *Shutruk-nahhunte* (*c.*1185–1155) to name his eldest son after his distinguished ancestor, and certainly Kutir-nahhunte, victor over the Kassites and conqueror of Babylon, did not betray his father's expectations.

King Shilhak-Inshushinak, a pious ruler imbued with a sense of the past, also preserved for posterity a sacred inscription of Kuter-Nahhunte I; the inscription was discovered when he re-established the capital at Susa, and he restored it and returned it to Susa. The Akkadian inscription tells us that Kuter-Nahhunte I and his son Tempt-agun, Prince of Susa, had shown a special regard for the statue of the god Inshushinak, in that they consecrated to it, for the benefit of their lives, a temple and a paved processional approach (which would have led diagonally to the temple gate, in the Elamite fashion).

An Akkadian tablet of Tempt-agun I, Prince of Susa, has been discovered there, according to which he founded a temple in honour of the goddess Ishmekarab. It is a text which is one of the many indicating his strong family sense. For Tempt-agun built his temple specifically for the benefit of the following people : his father, the Grand Regent Kuter-Nahhunte; his uncle, the Viceroy Lila-irtash; himself; his younger brother

*Tempt-hisha-hanesh*; and finally his 'gracious mother' *Welkisha*. While the royal women did inherit the right of rule, they had to surrender its practical application to the male members of the family, with the unique exception of Silhaha's sister.

Subsequent Grand Regents form a dynasty that embraces twelve generations, but due to the absence of further source material, they remain for the most part mere names. I have shown the Eparti in a chronological table in the Appendix, with approximate dates and family relationships where available.

Throughout its history, the pendulum of power had swung incessantly to and fro between Elam and its unfriendly neighbours in Mesopotamia: now one was supreme, now another. During the first half of the second millennium, Mesopotamia had by and large been in control, and this is confirmed by the Akkadian influence in Susa demonstrated by the almost exclusive use of Babylonian in the texts. However, a new power gradually forced its way on to the stage of Near-Eastern politics: the *Kassites*. The famous first dynasty came to its end after the retreat of the Hittites, when *Agun II*, King of the Kassites, occupied Babylon in 1593, thus putting an end to Babylonian supremacy over Elam. The problem is whether or not it was replaced by a Kassite tyranny. There are tablets – unfortunately undated – that bear witness to the presence of Kassites in Elam. Names such as *Ani-kilandi* in Huhnur, or *Rushupiash*, *Birgalzu*, and others, in Susa are Kassite. Even today, the name of the river *Kashghan* in northern Luristan recalls the *Kashshu* (Kassites). Naturally enough, no text states explicitly that the Kassites sounded the knell of the Eparti dynasty in Elam; in 1500 the sources simply dry up.

The mists over Elam are only dispelled by the victory over Susa gained by the Kassite King *Kurigalzu II*, who ruled in Babylonia (1345–1324). What happened in Elam in the preceding one hundred and fifty years? We have no idea. The end of the Eparti dynasty is shrouded in a mystery as profound as that which surrounds the downfall of the earlier dynasties of

99

Awan and Simashki. And yet there is a recurring impression
of a Kassite 'dark age' over Elam which smothered all attempts
at the expression of patriotic feelings, feelings which were not
revived until the new dynasty of Pahir-ishshan in 1330 B.C.
and the great classical era of Elamite history. This will be dealt
with in Chapter VI.

# CHAPTER V

# *Law*

---

An examination of Elamite law follows naturally at this point, after the history of the Eparti, because almost all relevant sources date from this period; apart from the five hundred or so legal documents from the time of the Great Regents, only seven others have so far been discovered, and those are from the later Elamite period. The luck of the dig can hardly be alone responsible for this. The Eparti sources make it more likely that it was at this period, when Susiana came under Akkadian influences, that written records of judicial events were kept for the first time in Elam. The legal system of Elam had originally been purely *oral*, and the age-old oral execution of the law had stood firm beside the written practices that had been imported from Babylonia. The individuality of the Elamite legal system lay in the alternating preponderance and interaction of these two methods.

In any case, our Akkadian tablets are concerned almost exclusively with financial cases. It is only here and there that a ray of light illumines details of Elamite criminal law, in the shape of the penalties that awaited those who broke their agreements.

A certain case report, dating from the end of the Eparti period, enables us to gain some idea of Elamite civil law. It goes like this :

Two brothers are demanding the return of a plot of land from a certain Bêli, the son of their deceased adoptive uncle, and appear before the chancellor and a judge. But Bêli defends himself as follows:

The father of the two plaintiffs, Damqiya, had adopted my father as his brother. In accordance with the 'paths of justice' established by god Inshushinak and goddess Ishmekarab, which affirm that adoption as a brother is to be considered as brotherhood and adoption as a son to be considered as filiation, I have inherited the land that my father once received [from Damqiya].

The trial, which took place in 1570 B.C., seems to have caused widespread excitement throughout Susa; not only the chancellor (*teppir*) of the Prince of Susa and the judge, but also the city governor, the head of the police, and numerous inhabitants of Susa took part in the trial. An inventory was drawn up of what Damqiya and the brother of his own kin had inherited from their father, and of what these two brothers had shared between each other, on oath to Grand Regent *Tata* and Tempt-Agun II, Regent of Susa. 'The tablets relevant to this division of the inheritance were brought to the chancellor and the judge, and they and many inhabitants of Susa took note of them, and pronounced judgement in the trial of these two plaintiffs.' Bêli was allowed to keep the plot that his father had inherited from Damqiya as his adoptive brother, and so the appeal of the two plaintiffs was dismissed. The verdict is followed by a list of witnesses, twenty-three altogether; the list is headed by *Atkalshu*, the city governor, and by *Inshushinak-kashid*, the head of the police, and concludes with god Inshushinak, goddess Ishmekarab and the court clerk. The text ends by directing both plaintiffs to return peacefully to their parents' house.

The clay tablet bears a large seal impression, representing a god with a horned crown, standing on a ceremonial stool with his arms raised. The Akkadian superscription informs us that the man in the seal – probably the chancellor of the Prince of Susa – has left his seat of office in the centre of Susa in order to authenticate the tablet. The judgement of the gods Humban and Inshushinak shall fall upon him who contests the verdict, be he plaintiff or defender. 'May the sceptre of the goddess Ishmekarab fall upon the head of him who destroys this document, on the command of the gods Inshushinak and Nahhunte.'

Let us now examine some features of this trial in greater detail.

In the text, the so-called 'paths of justice' of the gods Inshushinak and Ishmekarab are mentioned, while in other texts Inshushinak alone is referred to as the originator of these 'paths of justice' or guide-lines, and no other deities appear as law-givers. Among the people, the phrase 'paths of justice' was understood to mean simply that the laws had been given by the priests, as is shown by the not uncommon reference to a 'path of justice laid down by the Temple of Inshushinak'. However, ancient Elam possessed not only this 'canon law' of the temple, but also a secular law. The rulers of that period figure as its originators. However, it would be idle to attempt a clear-cut distinction between divine and secular law in Elam. It is true that Elamites viewed certain precepts as emanating from the gods, in particular from the god Inshushinak (at any rate in Susa) with the occasional co-operation of the goddess Ishmekarab (later Ishnikarab). But these legal precepts were by no means solely concerned with religious law; the divine 'paths of justice' also dealt with such secular questions as adoption, the apportionment of inheritances, the sale of property, the harvesting of crops, loans, the execution of agreed punishments, and so on. Those 'paths of justice' which had not been delineated by the gods were considered simply as the work of the current ruler; under the Grand Regents this would have been the dual supremacy of the Grand Regent himself and the Prince of Susa.

Of course, the rulers of Elam were not content simply to preserve existing laws under their own name; they added new ones. This is certainly true of Attahushu, Prince of Susa in 1810, as well as for the Grand Regent *Pala-ishshan* and his Prince of Susa in about 1560 B.C. We do not know whether or not the Elamite law was completely formulated at that time, but it seems unlikely; however, individual sections of the legal system seem to have been codified, and a tablet, much fragmented, has been found in Susa which deals with the Elamite law of property.

Probably those 'paths of justice' that claim divine provenance are part of the very earliest Elamite legal system, a system expanded by other laws of custom and by those proclaimed *ad hoc*. But there was never a distinction between divine and secular law; it was rather that the Elamites considered all law, even the secular, as rooted in the divine. The ruler and the deity worked as a team; we can see this in a later Elamite inscription, which remarks: 'The law that god Inshushinak and King Shutruk-nahhunte (II) have given . . .'

During those periods when Mesopotamia was politically supreme over Elam, it may be that foreign law was also valid, at least in Susiana. Several tablets dating from between 1670 and 1650 mention 'paths of justice' of the kingdom of Babylon, and it seems likely that the famous Code of Hammurabi was accepted in Elam, even if only to complement the native laws of custom. An Elamite basalt statue (Plate 27), portraying an unknown Grand Regent before the throne of the sun-god Nahhunte, looks very like an imitation of the stele of Hammurabi.

An important feature of Elamite law was its intimate connection with the numinous. We have already established the Elamite expression for this power as a *kiten* in Chapter III; whereas the *kiten* of the god Humban ensured the divine protection of the king, that of the god Inshushinak was primarily effective in legal pronouncements, particularly in Susa. In Huhnur in Anshan, Inshushinak was replaced by the local god

Ruhurater. In the Susa tablets, the treaty-breaker is warned that he will lose the protective power, the *kiten*, of Inshushinak, and this is a way of expressing the outlawing of the guilty party. Not uncommonly, the text adds laconically: 'He dies.' The threat of outlawry is often couched in the following terms: 'He is driven out from the jurisdiction of deity and kingship!' It appears at its most explicit in a text contemporary with Hammurabi (1792–1750): '[The treaty-breaker] is expelled from the jurisdiction of Silhaha, Sirktuh, Siwe-palar-huhpak [then Grand Regent], and of Kuduzulush [then Prince of Susa]. God Inshushinak, King of Susa [will annihilate him].' It is significant that this text even invokes two Eparti who were no longer alive, Silhaha and Sirktuh; this indicates that dead rulers possessed the power to curse and provides further proof of the Elamite belief in a life after death. Humban and Nahhunte appear on occasion with Inshushinak as gods of punishment; so much is clear from the seal impression on the trial tablet. All these threats reveal the indissoluble unity of divine and secular law.

However, the Elamite word *kiten*, as we have already suggested, did not only bear the abstract meaning of 'magical protection of the deity', but also the concrete one of 'taboo emblem'. The sanction: 'He has forfeited the protective power of the god Inshushinak' is literally: 'He has touched the *kiten* of Inshushinak.' The explanation is probably that the treaty-breaker was brought into contact with the taboo emblem of the god, and finally, supposing that this desecration did not prove lethal as a result of psychological distress, led to execution. In this connection I should perhaps also mention the threat: 'he shall pass by the statue of the god,' with its implication: 'And he will not survive that.' Inshushinak's taboo emblem was probably an eagle with outspread wings.

By extension from the concrete meaning of taboo emblem, *kiten* could also apply to the temple area in which the emblem was set up and therefore effective. There exists a treaty which tell us that the parties in disagreement were amicably reconciled 'at Susa in the *kiten* of the god Inshushinak'. This brings us to the question of *where* Elamite trials were conducted.

The sources are very uncommunicative on this point but do make it clear that the majority of Elamite trials took place in the temple grove of the sun-god Nahhunte. In complement to Inshushinak the law-giver, Nahhunte is the Elamite god of the execution of the law, and he in particular was responsible for trade; he established a rate of interest, standardized weights, and embarked on capitalist negotiations with mortal business-men in commercial partnerships. Nahhunte's sacred grove stood on the acropolis on the artificial hill in the north-west corner of Susa. A tablet remarks that a defendant and his opponent 'climb up' to judgement; after the acquittal, the latter was allowed to descend it once more. As it is often stated that proceedings took place 'in the *kiten* of Inshushinak', we can assume that his sign or taboo emblem was either brought in for the trial in the grove of Nahhunte, or was permanently set up there.

In our trial, the presidency was taken, you may remember, not by the judge but by the chancellor, most probably the minister of Tempt-agun II, Prince of Susa, who occupied this position under his father *Tata* (*c.* 1600–1580), and under Tata's brother *Atta-merra-halki* (*c.* 1580–1570), but who never became Grand Regent himself. A text from Huhnur also mentions a *teppir* (chancellor) as presiding over the court; he can only have been the chancellor of the then Prince of Huhnur. In Elam, presidency in civil proceedings of the second instance was taken by the chancellors of the princes of the individual provinces, with the help of a judge. In preliminary hearings, it was these judges alone who pronounced sentences; the chancellors only added their voices in appeal proceedings (*hashlut* in Elamite). However, it was always possible – as indeed it always has been in the East – to make a direct approach to the princes, over the heads of judge and chancellor: a matter of influence and perhaps of bribery. As one text has it: '[such and such] have gone to *Tempt-raptash* about the garment that they left me as a pledge, and he sent the chief of police to me, who has locked me here into my house.' This will refer to Tempt-raptash, Prince of Susa under the Grand Regent *Kuter-Silhaha I* in 1630 B.C.

It is significant that civil proceedings in Elam were entrusted to secular judges alone; priests are never more than witnesses in court. Our trial, which took place in the seat of the sun-god in the sacred grove, was exceptional in that, apart from chancellor and judge, the town governor and the head of police also took part. And it is equally unusual for the list of witnesses to be headed by these two municipal dignitaries. For the ancient laws of Elamite justice laid down that the list of witnesses should always begin with Nahhunte and Inshushinak, in that order; only occasionally was it reversed. Since these were considered the two divine rulers over the kingdoms of light and darkness, they were always included in the texts in the final count at the end of the list. In Huhnur, the place of the god Inshushinak was, logically enough, taken by the local god Ruhurater.

Witnesses played an overwhelmingly important role in Elamite law. Their very number is usually impressive, as high as forty-two. Only in the records of one tablet is the testimony of Nahhunte and Inshushinak alone sufficient, without mortals; otherwise the minimum appears to have been two mortals in addition to the gods. The majority of the texts mention between five and twenty witnesses.

The texts from Susa and Huhnur regularly contain penal clauses of a quite different character which give us some inkling of Elamite *criminal law*. Typical of Elam and so atypical of Babylon are (*a*) the threat of severe mutilation and (*b*) special treatment intended as a malediction of the treaty-breaker. Whoever commits perjury will have his 'hand and tongue cut off'. In addition, he commonly had to pay reparations, ranging from half a pound of silver and about eight hundredweight of corn to about sixty pounds of silver. And that was not all. A perjurer, even if he had only sworn by the ruler, had to forfeit the *kiten* of the god Inshushinak, thus losing his peace and his life at a blow. Infringement of an oath sworn by the ruler resulted not only in secular punishment but in explicit religious repercussions. As P. Koschaker says: 'The unity of secular and divine justice can scarcely be outlined more clearly.'

Where adoptions, inheritances and gifts were concerned, the usual punishment – in addition to the execration of god and ruler – was death by drowning. The penal code says of the perjurer: 'He shall go into the water; may the river-god Shazi shatter his skull in the tumultuous whirlpool. May the sceptre of god and king smite his head. May he be expelled from the kingdom of god and king.'

There is an interesting text from Huhnur, which contains an example of a verdict by oath and by ordeal through water. Ten women confirm that another woman, the plaintiff, received a gift from a certain man, who denied it. The court orders the plaintiff to submit to divine judgement in the river. If she sinks in the Karun, the defendant has won his case, but if she survives, the defendant must make good the gift. But even so he has to face no punishment for his earlier denial of the gift. Unfortunately, we are not told whether or not the woman Ayinlungu accepted the divine judgement, and if so, whether or not she perished miserably in the river. But it is significant that not even her ten witnesses were enough to verify her claim in the eyes of the law. In financial matters, the Elamite regard for women, otherwise so striking, appears to have faded.

Finally, the legal *standing* of women still remains to be explained.

Our sources indicate that Elamite women had gained a considerable measure of equality in the early Babylonian period, in contrast to their earlier position in the third and fourth millennia, when brothers were favoured at the expense of their sisters. As a patriarchal legal system won acceptance, resulting in the inheritance passing solely to the children, so the position of Elamite women improved. From then on, sons and daughters had equal rights of inheritance. In deeds of apportionment, women are to be found as well as men; indeed, they were sometimes the sole heirs. Women were allowed to appear as witnesses in court and we have already met them as plaintiffs as well as in the dock. Clay contract-tablets bear the imprint of their finger-nails next to those of their male co-signatories.

The following case is typical of the position of Elamite women :

A married daughter inherited her father's complete estate on his death. Her husband protested because the property was not a joint bequest and he therefore had no control over it, but his wife opposed this. She affirmed, in writing and under oath : 'You are my husband, you are my son, you are my heir, and our daughter will love and cherish you.' Her husband was content with this, and wisely refrained from pursuing his attempts to have the bequest transferred to himself. The sworn testimony of his wife endowed him with a power of decree which would hardly have been granted to him in court.

There is a further relevant tablet which states that a father had given his daughter a field; she bequeathed it to her daughter, and she to hers, who then sold it. From this it appears that in personal property there was a right of inheritance through the female line, comparable to the right of succession in the ruling house of Elam, which propagated itself through the distaff side. But Elamite man, as revealed in the tablets, usually displayed concern for the woman's welfare and often gave preference to his female relatives.

In one of these tablets, the dying father leaves his property to his children in equal shares, but he names his daughter *before* his son. In another text, a husband gives his wife a garden, and makes a point of adding specifically that she may keep the garden even if he were to separate from her. Similar concern inspires an Elamite who, on his death-bed, leaves all his property to his wife to enjoy for the rest of her life; but on her death, only those sons may inherit who have treated their mother with love and consideration. Paternal favour of the daughter emerges in a will in which the testator bequeathes all his property to his daughter although he had several sons and two wives (polygamy seems to have existed). 'As long as I am still alive, she (the daughter) will care for me, and, when I die, she shall bring sacrifices for the dead.' Those relatives who ignored these last injunctions were to be destroyed by the river-god Shazi, forfeit hand and tongue, pay four pounds of silver, and lose the *kiten* of the god Inshushinak. The sixteen witnesses to the will include four women.

I shall quote here one last relevant text dating from the time of the Grand Regent Atta-merra-halki (1580–1570 B.C.), in which a man makes over all his goods to his wife. He explains it thus: 'because she has looked after him and worked for him . . .' Nor is he content with these only precautions for the future comfort of his helpmeet: the sons may only inherit on condition that they stay with their mother and care for her.

All these texts, though couched in dry legal jargon, confirm the elevated social and administrative position of Elamite women. Under these somewhat unusual circumstances it is only fitting that an Elamite woman once rose to be a ruler of Susiana: Silhaha's famous sister, the ancestral mother of the Grand Regents.

# CHAPTER VI

# *The Classical Period (c. 1300-1100 B.C.)*

The final and the most terrible event of the Kassite 'dark ages' in Elam was the conquest of Susa by Kurigalzu II, who ruled Babylon from 1345–1324. A Babylonian chronicle informs us that *Hurpatila*, then 'King of Elam', and otherwise totally unknown, challenged the Kassite king. But Hurpatila was beaten; Kurigalzu, in a lightning campaign, overcame the whole of Susiana, a victory which he celebrated in the capital, where he dedicated his statue to an acropolis temple, with the inscription: 'Kurigalzu, King of the nations, the tyrant of Susa and Elam, the destroyer of Warahshi.'

The attack, as so often in the past, was launched from Babylon across the north-western mountains by Kabir-Kuh and down on to the plain of Susiana, and, as ever, it was Warahshi, Elam's ally, that bore the brunt of the first assault. In 1330 Kurigalzu, laden with booty, returned to Mesopotamia. But his luck soon changed. A new ruling house had arisen in Elam; its founder is identified by later sources as a certain *Ige-halki*. Apparently, as had happened at the beginning of the Eparti, the dynasty of the Igehalkids was only confirmed by the accession of the eldest son of its founder; he was *Pahir-ishshan I*, who reigned from 1330–1310. Our only information

about him is to be found on a stele which was brought to
Susa a hundred and fifty years later by King Shutruk-nahhunte
and there inscribed. Sadly, the inscription is nowhere free from
damage, added to which it is almost incomprehensible. If I
have understood the passage right, it describes Pahir-ishshan
as the prince 'who has established the peace of Elam'. It says
that Pahir-ishshan, like the Grand Regents Siwe-palar-huhpak
and Pala-ishshan before him, brought in certain plunder, about
which we still know nothing; he hid it in Ayahitek, where
Shutruk-nahhunte had found the stele. This would indicate that
Ayahitek was the seat of the new dynasty of the Igehalkids; I
further suggest that it lay in the mountains of Anshan that
bordered Susiana to the east – to be precise, near modern
Isfahan.

In keeping with the laws of succession, Pahir-ishshan was
followed by his younger brother *Attar-kittah*, whose rule may
have been from about 1310–1300 B.C. He also took plunder,
but hid it, according to the inscription, not in Ayahitek, but in
Susa, in the Temple of Inshushinak. And indeed, French
archaeologists have found two maces there, consecrated by
Attar-kittah. On one of them he refers to himself as 'King
of Anshan and Susa': this is the first time since Epart and
Silhaha, five hundred years earlier, that this uniquely Elamite
royal title is to be found. From now on it is to be *de rigeur*
for almost all rulers of Elam's classical period.

Attar-kittah was succeeded in 1300 by his son *Humban-
numena*. In the eyes of posterity, he stands out as one of the
great Igehalkids, even though the famous Silhaha had been his
ancestor. It is odd that the only Elamite text to concern itself
with Humban-numena should hail not from Susa but
from Liyan; the fulcrum of the power of the Igehalkids was no
longer in the north of Susiana as it had been under earlier
dynasties, but had shifted to the east and south.

Humban-numena had erected a temple to the 'great goddess'
in Liyan, and in the inscription he calls upon not only Humban and Kiririsha but also the 'benevolent gods of Liyan'. He

continues: 'I am Humban-numena, son of Attar-kittah, expander of my kingdom, monarch of Elam, ruler of Elam, governor of Elam, King of Anshan and Susa.' The next sentence confides: 'God Humban loved me for my mother's sake, and has granted my request.' Might this be yet another parallel with the earlier Eparti? If so, the 'gracious mother', Silhaha's sister, would correspond in our case to a sister of the Kings Pahir-ishshan and Attar-kittah. In any event Humban-numena claims that his mother enjoyed a position of particular favour with the god Humban.

Further on, we read that 'a healthy life was granted to me. God Inshushinak preserved the monarchy for me.' Then the author of the inscription turns to its dedication in Liyan, and mentions two women by name. The first, *Mishimruh*, was perhaps his 'gracious mother', the other presumably his wife. 'For the sake of my life,' writes Humban-numena, 'for that of Mishimruh and that of Rishap-la, I have erected and set up in the confines of the old ruined temple a high temple, which I have dedicated to God Humban, to Kiririsha the goddess, and to the benevolent gods.' Then he boldly adds the following request: 'May Humban, Kiririsha and the benevolent gods grant me eternal life! I prayed for the throne – may they lead me to it in good health!' Humban-numena's prolonged and stable rule in Elam clearly laid the foundation-stone for peace and prosperity. There is never a whisper of quarrels with the Kassites in Babylonia; the country thrived, riches flooded into the royal treasure-houses and allowed his son, the next king, *Untash-napirisha*, to embark on a unique programme of architectural development.

Untash-napirisha came to the throne in 1275 B.C. His name means '(*un*) me (*tash*) helped the great god (*napi-risha*)'. This is the god Humban, and for this reason his name used to be read as Untash-Humban. But the holy name of Humban was clearly already taboo in the early second millennium and thereafter was almost invariably disguised as the Sumerian word sign *dingir.gal* (*napirisha* in Elamite) meaning 'great god'. As a result of this, it has even been doubted whether the 'great god' referred to Humban at all – but this must be wrong. This taboo was relaxed in the later period, and not only does the name Humban-untash ('god Humban helped me') occur in the seventh century written out in full, but we also find several proper names at that time where Humban alternated with *dingir.gal* (*napirisha* in Elamite). So Humban will have been the 'great god' of the Elamites.

The obscurity involved in the name Untash-napirisha conveys some idea of the awe with which the Elamites held Humban as their supreme god; indeed, as we have seen, the *kiten* of Humban was counted as the special prerogative of the kings. Further, Untash-napirisha was without doubt a deeply religious man. It was no chance that made him responsible for the construction of the most impressive manifestation of Elamite religious art, the ziggurat at Choga Zambil (already mentioned, in particular in Chapter III).

Untash-napirisha was very probably a contemporary of the Assyrian King *Shalmaneser I* (1274–1245), and under his rule Elam of the Igehalkids enjoyed a golden age. His rule gives the impression of great power and also of benevolent wisdom. It is true that a hundred years later, Shilhak-Inshushinak was to bring in Elam's most superficially glorious era, but Untash-napirisha seems to have been his superior as a personal ruler. It is certain that Elam flourished under him more than at any other period. He devoted his long reign principally to building projects within his own boundaries, and to religion. He seems to have made only one venture into the realm of external politics. During his rule, four Kassite kings succeeded each other in neighbouring but hostile Mesopotamia, while Untash-napirisha quietly observed the continuing collapse of Babylonia. However, when the time seemed ripe, he launched a surprise attack.

We know of this attack from a fragment of the statue of a Babylonian weather-god, Immeriya, that was found in Susa;

it had been removed as plunder by Untash-napirisha and inscribed in Akkadian. The beginning of the decisive third line is missing: there is room for one sign and then comes [ ... ]-*li-ia-ash*. For a long time this has been completed as *Kashtiliash*, which would mean that the statue originally belonged to the Kassite king *Kashtiliash IV* (1242–1234). However, Erica Reiner has proposed the much more plausible reading [*Tup*]-*liash*, which exactly fits the space, as *tup* is a single sign. Tupliash is the Kassite name for the territory of Eshnunna (to the north of Baghdad); if, as seems likely, Untash-napirisha plundered the statue from there, he would have pressed through to Mesopotamia across friendly Warahshi and past Dêr – now Badra – and so laid waste Eshnunna. Immeriya, embodied in the statue, was in fact the god who protected Eshnunna. Although the earlier reading of [Kashti]liash must now be taken as wrong, it is not impossible that Untash-napirisha did in fact lead an attack on this same king; it was under him that Babylonia's power weakened most perceptibly.

Untash-napirisha was responsible for a resurgence of Elamite patriotism due to Elam's liberation from Babylonian tyranny. However he continued to profit from the culture of Mesopotamia. This is proved not only by the inscription referred to above on the plundered statue and by any number of Untash-napirisha's other Akkadian inscriptions, but also by the presence in what had been an exclusively Elamite pantheon of several Babylonian deities, who enjoyed equal privileges. The king dedicated temples and chapels to these foreign gods just as he did to the Elamite ones.

Under Untash-napirisha, Elamite art reached its peak, in particular in architecture and carving. We shall go into this in further detail in Chapter VIII; here we shall confine ourselves to those architectural achievements which illuminate his personality as a ruler.

The huge ziggurat at Choga Zambil was constructed not only in an extensive sacred precinct, the *Siyankuk*, but also in a town, newly planned by the king. It bore his name: *Al-Untash* or *Dur-Untash*, from the Akkadian *alu* 'town', or *duru*, 'citadel'. It was conceived on the grand scale. The ziggurat, with its five steps, was surrounded by an inner wall; the plans provided temples for twenty-two deities between that and a second wall, but only thirteen were built; Untash-napirisha's foundation was not completed before his death, and strangely enough his successors never added to it.

The royal palace and the town itself were sited in the space between the second, middle wall, and a third external one (Plate 9); this outer wall was over four thousand metres long. Untash-napirisha protected his work with curses inscribed on countless bricks, mostly in Elamite but sometimes in Akkadian : 'He who takes in a charge [?] the walls of the sacred precinct, who makes a breach in them, steals the inscribed bricks, burns the door beams, and opens the gates to the approaching foes, may he be struck by the punishing sceptre of Humban, Inshushinak and Kiririsha. May he have no descendants under the sun.'

In a few sentences, the king summarizes the essentials of the building and its dedication to the deity : 'After I had obtained the building materials, I erected here 'Untash-town' and the sacred precinct. I enclosed it in an inner and an outer wall. I built a high temple, unlike those put up by earlier kings, and dedicated it to the gods Humban and Inshushinak, the protectors of the holy precinct. May my building and work be offered to them in dedication. May the grace and justice of Humban and Inshushinak hold sway here.'

The king must have encountered great difficulty in providing his new town with water. It is true that the Diz was only one and a half kilometres away, but the river-bed was about sixty metres lower than the town itself. The springs contained only brackish water, as the French archaeologists discovered to their dismay, and in any case only at a depth of fourteen metres. The puzzle of how the king solved the problem was given an astonishing solution by R. Ghirshman : Untash-napirisha diverted good water from the Karkheh along a canal more than fifty kilometres in length. Far north of Susa, the canal branched off from the main river, and ran southwards for about thirty-five kilometres to somewhere near what is now Haft Tepeh; there it turned to the east and ran straight to Choga Zambil. A considerable portion has been preserved at Haft Tepeh under the incorrect name of the Darius Canal; it was incorporated without difficulty into the irrigation scheme of the new sugar-cane plantations. The bed of the Untash-napirisha canal was about one and a half metres wide; its banks about seven. What can the work-force involved in such a project have been, in the thirteenth century B.C.? Naturally, the canal served to irrigate other fields along its course before reaching the town. However, a second problem faced the royal irrigation experts in that the town was still some metres above the surface of the canal. And so they constructed a large tidal basin, still in immaculate condition today. The fissures in the brick-work of the walls were carefully filled with bitumen, and nine ducts on the bottom of the basin connected it with a smaller basin inside the town wall; to feed it, the Elamite technicians made extensive use of the principle of communicating tubes.

The completion of this vast undertaking was commemorated by Untash-napirisha in a Babylonian inscription, whose correct interpretation is the work of Maggie Rutten. 'I, Untash-napirisha, son of Humban-numena, King of Susa and Anshan, have fulfilled my heart's desire and built a canal, the "fame of my name", exercising my royal power, for my life and for my well-being, for many days and for years, and have dedicated it to the gods Humban and Inshushinak, protectors of the sacred precinct.'

However, 'Untash-town' never appears to have been more than a holy town, to which the king and his court paid occasional visits; Susa remained unchallenged as the capital of the kingdom of Elam, benefiting also from the king's architectural proclivities. It is plain that he built another ziggurat in Susa, also with a high temple. It was in this shrine that he dedicated his lime-stone statue, whose Elamite inscription is in parts obscure to the point of incomprehensibility, in the present state of our knowledge. The beginning is clear enough: 'The gods Humban and Inshushinak loved me.' Then follows a sentence which appears to be concerned with the inhabitants of Susa. It continues: 'In the high temple to which they led me and accompanied me, I received you and I set myself up on high.' This may well mean that the statue of the king was accompanied in a ceremonial procession by the people of Susa to the topmost temple room of the ziggurat, where it was set up. There, either in person during worship or represented by his statue at other times, the king received Humban and Inshushinak, the chief deities, who were either paying a visit to the high temple or were considered to be in permanent residence there.

It is unfortunate that Untash-napirisha volunteers no further family details in his inscriptions: we only know about his wife from her statue in bronze (Plate 29) and unfortunately the head is missing. The queen's attitude is one of majestic repose: hands crossed, she prays. A richly embroidered garment is wrapped closely round breast and shoulders; the skirt girding her hips falls past her feet to the ground. An inscription in Elamite gives us her name: 'I am Napir-asu, wife of Untash-napirisha,' and the claim is carefully repeated. *Napir-asu* may mean 'the moon-like'. The identification is followed by a curse on any man who steals the statue, who melts it down, alters the queen's inscription or erases her name. 'May the punishing sceptre of Humban, Inshushinak and Kiririsha fall on his head! He shall make no name for himself under the sun and shall have no descendants. I pray: may my mistress the great goddess bring this upon him.' We are not told who this mistress is; perhaps Pinikir or Narunte. The inscription ends with a list of the sacrifices which Napir-asu made daily.

The statue was found in Susa, but other clues about the queen have come to light in 'Untash-town' (Choga Zambil). The remains of palaces have been exposed between the middle and outer walls. The plans of their foundations by P. Auberson can be seen next to each other in Figure 32. The palace on

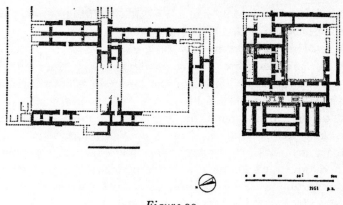

*Figure 32*

the left, 116 metres long and 58 metres wide, was, on Ghirshman's illuminating suggestion, Untash-napirisha's harem. It is possible that Napir-asu was mistress of this extensive construction. The building on the right was presumably the king's living quarters; excavations have revealed a number of fine ivories in one room. Under the rooms on the western side of the courtyard, a carefully concealed flight of steps led six metres down into subterranean vaults. In one of these a skeleton was discovered, lying on a brick funerary bed, and also the remains of two charred corpses. In a neighbouring vault, heaps of ashes were discovered on the floor in groups of two, four and five. So far, this is the only evidence that cremation was practised in Elam. It seems likely that it was to these subterranean vaults that the mortal remains of King Untash-napirisha, of his queen, Napir-asu, and of other members of his family were consigned; and also that this type of burial was reserved for the royal house.

Untash-napirisha, who had no son, was succeeded in 1240 by his nephew *Unpatar-napirisha*. His father, *Pahir-ishshan II*, brother to Untash-napirisha, may have been Viceroy. We know nothing of Unpatar-napirisha except his name; his rule was brief, and in 1235 he was followed by his younger brother

119

*Kiten-Hutran.* His full name was *Kiten-Hutran-u-tash,* 'the magic protection of God Hutran helped me'.

Kiten-Hutran seems to have been one of those rulers whose interest inclined more towards military glory than to the erection of sacred buildings and the composition of inscriptions. In other words, details of his private life are nearly as scanty as those of Unpatar-napirisha. He is simply mentioned in two later king lists as King of Elam. Our only information on his military activities is to be found in sources from Mesopotamia, a land on which he plainly left a permanent impression. It was unfortunate for this bellicose king that he was matched by an equally aggressive opponent : *Tukulti-Ninurta I*, King of Assyria. The son of Shalmaneser I, he ruled for thirty-seven years, from 1242 to 1206, and during this period he succeeded in extending his influence to the south as far as Babylon. It was in this same territory that Kiten-Hutran met him on two occasions.

The Elamite king was basically concerned to gain control of the border country between Elam and Babylonia, Dêr and Ulaiash (the present-day territory round Badra and Mandali in Iraq). After the death of the Kassite King Kashti-liash IV in 1231 B.C., the Assyrian king had established as successor to the Babylonian throne one of his satellites, Ellil-nadin-shumi. In 1226 Kiten-Hutran seized his opportunity and staged a sudden irruption into Mesopotamia. The Elamite army crossed the Tigris and conquered Nippur in central Babylonia; its inhabitants were slain to a man. The king then turned north, crossed the Tigris once again, and occupied Dêr, whose townsfolk were taken prisoner and whose famous temple was destroyed. The Kassite King of Babylonia was forced to flee.

However, almost at once Tukulti-Ninurta brought Babylonia once more under Assyrian sway. His first step in 1226 was to install the Kassite Kadashman-harbe as his vassal in Babylon; a year and a half later he replaced him by Adad-shum-iddin. He reigned for five years, from 1224 to 1219, during which time Kiten-Hutran refrained from any further exploits. His next attack could not be risked until Adad-shum-nasir's accession to the throne in 1218 (his rule lasted till 1189). Once again he crossed the Tigris, captured Isin, and pressed on to the north right up to Marad, west of Nippur. Laden with booty, he returned unmolested to Elam.

But, as before, the Assyrian king was not slow in taking his revenge. Tukulti-Ninurta marched victorious to the 'lower sea', or Persian Gulf, and occupied the Elamite coast, thus menacing Susiana from the south. We do not know what happened next; it is only certain that Kiten-Hutran vanished abruptly from the historical scene, and with him the dynasty of the Igehalkids. There may have been a period of temporary internal chaos in Elam; in any case a new dynasty soon appeared.

The father of the new ruling house was called *Hallutush-Inshushinak*, which means: 'God Inshushinak was friendly to the land.' His origins remain obscure, nor do we know whether he was related to the Igehalkids. All the evidence suggests that the new royal house sprang from the far south-east of Anshan, near modern Fahlian and further east as far as Persepolis/ Shiraz. We know nothing of his achievements, only that he reigned from 1205 to 1185 B.C.

But we do know something of his son, *Shutruk-nahhunte* ('he who is led rightly by the sun-god') (1185–1155). It is after him that the royal house is known as the Shutrukids, and he, his son *Shilhak-Inshushinak* and Untash-napirisha must be accounted the three greatest kings of Elam.

The historian is grateful to Shutruk-nahhunte because he, unlike Kiten-Hutran, has bequeathed to us an enormous number of inscriptions; without question, others still await discovery, hidden in Elamite soil, particularly at Deh-e nou, once Hupshen (Plate 3). One text was even found at Liyan (Bushire); this would indicate that Shutruk-nahhunte exercised a firm control over the whole of Elam, and that is indeed the only explanation of his military victories in Mesopotamia. The same text reveals that the temple to Kiririsha built by Humban in

Liyan was already in ruins; Shutruk-nahhunte took it upon himself to repair it.

We have already referred to another of his inscriptions, the stele that he plundered in Ayahitek (Isfahan?). Its poor condition and difficult Elamite vocabulary make it, too, almost totally unintelligible although it could be most revealing. In it, the king tells us that he has had the stele moved from Ayahitek to Susa. He goes on : 'I am Shutruk-nahhunte, son of Hallutush-Inshushinak, King of Anshan and Susa, increaser of my kingdom. None of the previous kings recognized the place [of the stele] for his horned warriors.' We learn here in passing that the contemporary Elamite soldiers wore horned helmets; such horned warriors are indeed depicted on a somewhat later bronze relief from Susa (Plate 31). 'I, Shutruk-nahhunte, have called upon my god Inshushinak, because he helps me; he has granted my plea and has shown my horned warriors the place.'

As far as I can make out, the king states further that he picked up in Tahirman a scout of the Shala people, and marched to Teeda, which god Inshushinak captured for him. The god also advanced to Hashmar and occupied Shahnam. It is true that there is a mountain and a pass called Hashmar, where the Diyala breaks through the Djebel Hamrin into the Iraqi plain, but it is impossible that they are the same. None of the earlier kings, as Shutruk-nahhunte reiterates, knew the place of origin of the stele; and a man neither from Shala nor from Mimurash nor from Luppun (all equally unknown to us) could have shown him the way. When he questioned his father about the area, his father could remember nothing and could give him no information. This last remark is, if I have not misunderstood the text, quite remarkable; for his father, Hallutush-Inshushinak, cannot possibly still have been alive at the time. It seems possible that methods of 'interrogating the dead' were not unknown in Elam.

The inscription continues: 'I was received by Inshushinak my god, and after he had shown the place [of the stele] to my horned warriors through me, I took it into my protection and kept the vanquished land as my kingdom.' What its inhabitants once stole has been restored by him, Shutruk-nahhunte. Another excerpt asserts: 'O Inshushinak, thou my god! Since you helped me, I, Shutruk-nahhunte, armed with horns, took the earth into my protection.' It appears that the king took water, earth and embers from the lands he had conquered, and transferred these souvenirs of victory to Susa. The end of the inscription is mutilated and particularly obscure; it is however clear that the Elamite booty included thirty loads of copper and '2,455 weights of corn[?] for the camp granary'. 'In all I sent 3,415 horned warriors to Huhnur in the land of the stele' – such is the final sentence of the inscription. If Huhnur really means the area around what is now Izeh (Malamir), Shutruk-nahhunte could have risked crossing the Karun to advance upon the highlands near modern Isfahan. It is therefore possible that it is here that we must look for Ayahitek.

Shutruk-nahhunte's inscription reveals a characteristic trait which is recurrent in his inscriptions: he had a true collector's passion for memorial stones, a passion that endears him to the historian, for the king usually inscribed the steles himself, thus authenticating them. Hardly any other Elamite ruler brought as many inscriptions to Susa and dedicated them to the Temple of Inshushinak.

On one occasion, he found such a stele somewhere in the eastern mountains of Anshan. 'I do not know which king set it up,' he remarks on it. 'Since god Inshushinak was helping me, I appropriated it and brought it on the way to Susa, past Kutkin and Nahutirma. Because I love 'Untash-town' (Choga Zambil) on the Hithite (the Diz), I left the memorial stone there for five months[?] and travelled on.' The Elamite inscription is here very far from easy, and I cannot vouch for the accuracy of my translation. It seems that at the end of this time the stele was removed to Tikni, presumably by boat up the canal built by Untash-napirisha. Shutruk-nahhunte says that he also loved Tikni, so we can assume that the stele enjoyed a further period of repose here, in order to bring blessings upon the place. Tikni, according to the convincing suggestion of Ghirshman, is now Haft Tepeh; its Elamite foundations have been covered in by the offices of the sugar-cane plantation. And finally the stele arrived in Susa. 'For my well-being, I set up the memorial stone before my god Inshushinak, and to honour him have set his name upon it.'

On one of his visits to Untash-town, the king's fancy had been taken by a stele dedicated by Untash-napirisha in the sacred precinct or *Siyankuk*. He gazed thoughtfully at it for a while, and the result of this careful scrutiny was that this stele also embarked on the journey to Susa. The explanation given by this passionate collector is somewhat disarming: 'Untash-napirisha set up this stone in the sacred precinct. In accordance with the command of god Inshushinak, I, Shutruk-nahhunte, appropriated the stele and set it up before my god Inshushinak in Susa.' One is tempted to wonder how this command reached the king's ears.

The sacred court of the temple of Inshushinak, with its many steles and statues, became a veritable forest of stonework when the king desposited there the booty brought back from the expedition that he undertook against Babylonia in 1160.

The Kassite kingdom had at that period become so powerful that the Assyrian King *Ashshur-dan I* (1179–1133) had encountered no resistance in his attempts to incorporate several Babylonian border towns on the lower Zab into his kingdom. This was the signal to the Elamites to embark on a series of conquests of their own. In 1160, Shutruk-nahhunte, accompanied by his eldest son Kutir-nahhunte, broke out from Susa, crossed the Karkheh, and attacked Mesopotamia, presumably from Dêr (now Badra). Subsequent Babylonian reports still bear the traces of the terrible impression made by the Elamites, who 'rushed down from the mountains with horses and chariots.' The princes of Babylon were defeated; 'the warlike Elamite stole plunder from all the temples, he removed their possessions and took them to Elam.' It is unfortunate that little has survived of Shutruk-nahhunte's personal account of the expedition, but it is clear from fragments that the Elamite army captured many hundreds of Babylonian towns. In Babylon itself, the Elamite king routed the penultimate Kassite (Zababashum-iddina) from the throne, and nominated his own son Kutir-nahhunte as Regent of Babylonia.

Then Shutruk-nahhunte marched out in triumph from the capital. 'God Inshushinak helped me. I beat Akkad, appropriated the statue of Manishtusu and sent it to Elam.' He tells us this on the statue itself. In transferring it to Elam, he took his revenge after more than a thousand years on one of the traditional enemies of his country, the younger son of the great Sargon of Akkad.

From Akkad, he moved into neighbouring Sippar. 'God Inshushinak helped me, and so I overcame Sippar, and I appropriated the stele of Naram-Sin, kept it and sent it to Elam, and then I set it up before my god Inshushinak.' On this occasion, Shutruk-nahhunte was planning revenge on the grandson of Sargon the Great, on that very Naram-Sin whom we have already encountered as tyrant in Elam in 2280, when Hita was ruling in Awan. Naram-Sin's famous stele celebrated, in words and pictures, his victory over the mountain races in the Zagros, but now it had found its way into Shutruk-nahhunte's stele collection at Susa.

Shutruk-nahhunte imposed an enormous tribute on his conquered victims. The towns of Babylonia (an inscribed fragment mentions Dur-Kurigalzu, Upu, Dur-Sharrukin and Sippar) had to raise, among other things, 120 talents (about 3,600 kilograms) of gold and 480 talents (about 14,400 kilograms) of silver, a monstrous sum for the period. In Sippar, the obelisk bearing Hammurabi's famous Code fell into the conqueror's hands. In all innocence, Shutruk-nahhunte rendered an inestimable service to scholarship when he removed the monument; for this legal stele survived in Susa, unscathed, not only the attacking Assyrians in 646 B.C., but all the subsequent storms with which history battered Susiana. It is true that Shutruk-nahhunte had seven of the fifty-one legal columns chiselled away from the Akkadian code; but he never replaced them by an inscription of his own. The stele is now the pride of the Louvre collection.

After Shutruk-nahhunte had returned to Susa, probably still in 1160, to gloat over his collection of steles, Crown Prince Kutir-nahhunte was commanding a crack Elamite regiment in Babylonia. The position there was by no means secure, and so he had providently established a Kassite on the throne, *Ellil-nadin-ahhi*. As vassal to Elam, he was responsible for maintaining order. Later developments in Mesopotamia are to be deduced only from the important Babylonian king, Nebuchadnezzar I : he tells us that Shutruk-nahhunte had handed over the Babylonian command to 'his first-born son, Kutir-nahhunte'. But his crimes surpassed by far the misdoings of his forefathers. 'He thought evil against the land of Akkad, and installed one of my precedessors [in Babylon], Ellil-nadin-ahhi.' However, he, the last of the Kassite kings, very soon rebelled against his Elamite overlords. For three years Kutir-nahhunte had struggled with the refractory Babylonians, and then in 1157 he won a decisive victory. The last of the Kassite kings was forced – as was the last King of Ur III, 850 years earlier – to tread the path of Elamite exile.

Only Nebuchadnezzar gives us details :

> Kutir-nuhhunte grew wrath [against the Kassites], and like a deluge swept all the people of Akkad away. He turned Babylon and the other famous shrines into piles of rubble. He forced the great lord Marduk [Babylonia's chief deity] to rise from the throne of his majesty. He led the people of Akkad and Sumer captive into Elam. He also dragged Ellil-nadin-ahhi away, overthrew his kingdom, and ended his rule. He replaced him by one who was not of Babylonian origin but who was an enemy of Marduk.

Thus the year 1157 saw the end of Kassite rule and yet Elam's supremacy in Babylonia went by no means unchallenged. The sorrow and resentment which the Elamite outrage – in particular the removal of Marduk's statue – had aroused among the populace fostered a hot-bed of resistance from which sprang the foundations of the new dynasty established by the Babylonian, *Marduk-kabit-ahhshu* from Isin. His eighteen years of rule from 1156 to 1138 were bedevilled by constant Elamite irruptions and attacks; however, Elam never succeeded in overthrowing the second kingdom of Isin.

King Shutruk-nahhunte probably died a few years after the fall of the Kassite supremacy (1155). Since he was apparently survived by no brothers, his eldest son acceded to the throne in accordance with Elamite law. While still Prince of Susa, Kutir-nahhunte had embarked on the reconstruction of the Temple of Inshushinak in the capital. In an inscription from this period, in which he described himself simply as the 'beloved servant' of the god, without any secular titles, he tells us that the walls of the inner shrine were in ruins. So he commanded that they should be torn down and replaced by brick ones, which he had decorated with highly individual reliefs; however, the reconstruction was not completed before his death.

Kutir-nahhunte may have died as early as 1150. Later Babylonian records tell dreadful stories about his death: that his only son, Prince *Hutelutush-Inshushinak*, murdered his father with an iron dagger, a report that seems barely credible. This supposed patricide kept his uncle, the dead man's brother, by him throughout his long reign as Prince of Susa; after Kutir-nahhunte's death, this same uncle, *Shilhak-Inshushinak*, married the widow, *Nahhunte-utu*, mother of the supposed murderer. When Hutelutush-Inshushinak subsequently came to the throne himself, this alleged patricide described himself proudly as the son of Kutir-nahhunte *and* of Shilhak-Inshushinak. It could of course be claimed that these assertions, found in the inscriptions, are only manifestations of the most hypocritical cunning; but it is far more likely that Kutir-nahhunte died a natural death and that his nearest relatives then followed Elamite tradition by forming a still closer relationship with each other.

When Shilhak-Inshushinak, according to Elamite precedent, followed his elder brother Kutir-nahhunte to the throne in 1150, the last of the great kings of Elam had made their appearance in world history. He also kept Kutir-Nahhunte's only son, Hutelutush-Inshushinak, as Prince of Susa, equally in accordance with long-established laws.

Of all the Elamite kings, Shilhak-Inshushinak (which means 'strengthened by god Inshushinak') bequeathed by far the greatest number of inscriptions, nearly thirty, of which many are of a considerable length. Although large portions of these inscriptions remain obscure, the sheer quantity of the material means that much can be inferred from the context. Shilhak-Inshushinak continued the policy towards Babylonia that had been favoured by his predecessors, plaguing the lives of the first three kings of the second kingdom of Isin by repeated attacks on Mesopotamia; but the demands that this offensive policy made on Elamite resources were clearly excessive, for when the valiant Nebuchadnezzar rose to power in Babylonia, the wheel of fortune turned and Elam quickly lost her influence – but only after Shilhak-Inshushinak's death.

He reigned for nearly thirty years and so may have lived to see Nebuchadnezzar's accession in 1124. However, in this portrait of this last great ruler of Elam, I am now less concerned with the features of the victorious general than with those of the pious paterfamilias. His inscriptions reveal an uncommonly strong loyalty to family and to tradition – indeed to all his royal forbears. He participated wholeheartedly in their building activities in the sacred precinct at Susa, and it must have given him real pleasure to rebuild from the foundations the shrine of Inshushinak, and to profit by the occasion to preserve those of his predecessors' inscriptions which were still accessible. His father, Shutruk-nahhunte, had displayed a similar concern in the way he restored the Temple of Manzat, wife of Simut, in Susa; in the course of this he stumbled upon bricks bearing the inscriptions of earlier kings. 'I took this brick into my protection,' ran his report, 'and I have kept the names and the titles [of those rulers] here, and left what they wrote in the temple; then I added my name and incorporated the brick into the wall.'

It is to these archivist propensities of his son that we owe the only king lists from the Middle Elamite period. They are in one case the product of the many name-bricks of previous royal architects; the king added his own name to them and immured them again in the Temple of Inshushinak. Bricks of fourteen rulers survived, beginning with Hutran-tempt, the probable destroyer of the Sumerian dynasty of Ur III in 2006 B.C., through Epart and a whole succession of other Grand Regents, down to Humban-numena the Igehalkid. The other king list that has come down to us is the work of Shilhak-Inshushinak himself, who collected the names on one of his great steles.

These lists are to be prized as the fruits of Shilhak-Inshushinak's own labours; the royal archivist and historian clearly felt the need to set his own life and achievements in the larger framework of Elamite history. His catalogue comprises sixteen kings who had built on to the Temple of Inshushinak before him, and extends from Indattu-Inshushinak, Hutran-tempt's nephew, to his own elder brother Kutir-nahhunte. 'These earlier kings', says Shilhak-Inshushinak, 'have worked here in the shrine of Inshushinak. I have neither rejected nor altered their inscriptions, but have rewritten them and incorporated them in the Temple of Inshushinak.'

Such respect for the past and for his ancestors is matched by Shilhak-Inshushinak's concern for his near relations, which may claim to be unique. No Babylonian, Assyrian or Persian would have dreamt of composing inscriptions such as those that were the work of this man. It is true that the relief found in Qal'e-ye Toll, south of Izeh (Plate 17) can hardly originate from Shilhak-Inshushinak, but it will serve very well as an illustration of what we have been saying. The king and queen are greeting each other with respect, while two sons are standing on the left and two daughters on the right. In the whole of the ancient Near East, there is no comparable 'family portrait'.

Let us now examine more closely the written evidence of this Elamite family feeling. In many of the inscriptions, Shilhak-Inshushinak refers to his entire family by name. The list of his children varies in length, and this very variety enables us to arrange them in chronological order, since the longest must also be the latest. In one of these inscriptions, the king tells us that he has had the Temple of Inshushinak rebuilt of baked bricks, not only for the benefit of his own life, but for the lives of those people whom he then proceeds to enumerate by name and in order of precedence. This catalogue is, as one would expect, headed by Queen *Nahhunte-utu*, his brother's widow whom he had afterwards married, faithful to the Elamite royal custom. Nahhunte-utu, whose name may mean 'sun-womb', is described as his 'beloved spouse'. It is not impossible that she was his (and thus Kutir-nahhunte's) own sister.

She is followed by the princes and princesses in order of age. The list begins with Hutelutush-Inshushinak, even though he was in no way Shilhak-Inshushinak's own son but the son of his elder brother Kutir-nahhunte. That made no difference; the deciding factor was always that Hutelutush-Inshushinak was the *queen's* eldest son. It was the same privilege of position that ensured his subsequent accession, before Shilhak-In-shushinak's own sons. From the marriage between Shilhak-Inshushinak and Nahhunte-utu were born eight children : first two daughters (Ishnikarab-duri and Urutuk-Elhalahu), and then two sons, of which the first, Shilhina-hamru-Lagamar, was next in order of accession after his elder half-brother Hutelutush-Inshushinak – a right that was in fact exercised. But history has nothing to relate of the second son Kutir-napirisha. The fifth child was another daughter, Utu-e-hihhi-Pinikir ('I have dedicated her womb to Pinikir'); the sixth a son, Tempt-turkatash; the seventh a son, Lila-irtash; and the eighth a daughter, Par-Uli. Of all the nine princes and princesses in the inscription, she is the only one to merit a description: her father Shilhak-Inshushinak refers to her tenderly as 'my beloved daughter, my child of happiness' – in these words the nestling Par-Uli entered the history of Elam.

Shilhak-Inshushinak's deep sense of family feeling had its roots in his very Elamite piety. He, more than any other Elamite ruler, was concerned to build temples and to preserve them in good condition. On one occasion he tells us, not without satisfaction, that he has had altogether twenty 'grove-temples' put up in different parts of the country: to Humban, Pinikir and Lagamar, but above all to Inshushinak.

The king felt himself especially close to Inshushinak; when addressing him he speaks not just as a sovereign but as a man of piety who is hoping for support and encouragement from his god. This is why most of his inscriptions are dedicated to Inshushinak, the 'merciful lord who gave me his name'. Many prayers, usually subscribed to by his 'beloved spouse' Nahhunte-utu, are addressed to the god; they are constantly reiterated in inscriptions and yet they are never stereotyped. 'O Inshushinak, thou lord of my city, be merciful to me! I, Shilhak-Inshushinak, and Nahhunte-utu, have called on you in sacrifice. You have always answered our pleas – now grant our request!' Or, on his own behalf: 'Grant thou my plea, do thou what I say!'

However, the king did not rely solely on Inshushinak; on the contrary, he is confident that all the other gods are well-inclined towards him: 'May the gods of Elam, the gods of Anshan, and the gods of Susa effect our happiness, my own and that of Nahhunte-utu. May evil avoid the people of Susa!' This expresses on stone the hope that he will overcome his enemies. His appeals use expressions very similar to those coined five hundred years earlier by the Grand Regent Siwe-palar-huhpak, indicating the conservative Elamite character. 'O God Inshushinak, wipe out the enemy army! Trample underfoot their name and their kind! Burn, flay and roast them!

May fire consume the enemy, and may their allies hang on the gallows! Burnt and flayed, they shall lie at my feet in chains!'

These curses from Shilhak-Inshushinak take us back to the military expedition described above. It is clear that they were aimed only at Babylon, at the kings of the second kingdom of Isin; but they also suggest that the victories of his predecessors Shutruk-nahhunte and Kutir-nahhunte were by no means permanently effective. Elam's manpower was not sufficient to ensure this: at most it was isolated areas around the Zagros foothills that were intermittently under Elamite control. In Susa, it is true, fragments of a large number of Shilhak-Inshushinak's victory steles have been found, but unfortunately they provide no cohesive picture of his campaigns. One of these commemorative steles contains a formal war-report; however, it is badly mutilated and barely comprehensible. Since we are unable to trace the king's individual expeditions, a general view must suffice.

In all probability, most of his offensives were launched through the terrible and strategic pass at Dêr (Badra) into Mesopotamia, after which he marched in a roughly northerly direction. The first area to capitulate was round the Diyala, before the 'gate of Asia', on the military road from Babylon to the Iranian highlands. The Elamite troops pressed forward along it and captured Yalman (now Hulwan). As his father had done, Shilhak-Inshushinak overcame the town of Karindash (Kerend). It is sad that only a few lines still remain of the stele celebrating this victory, but even they give us an idea of how the Elamite 'horned soldiers' rampaged through enemy territory: 'All the descendants of the King of Karindash, his wives and his concubines and his family, were herded together and led into exile and [...]' At this point the inscription breaks off, and the rest is left to our imagination. Shilhak-Inshushinak probably returned to Susiana over the mountains of Luristan, after once more establishing the much-disputed military road as an Elamite possession.

Subsequent campaigns extended from the Diyala area to the

north. The Elamites took possession of the mountains of Ebeh (Jebel-hamrin) and captured Madga (now Tuz-khurmatli). Shilhak-Inshushinak had thus entered the boundaries of the Assyrian territory, but with his victory over Urgarsallu near the lower Zab, he hounded the Assyrian King Ashshur-dan from the same territory that the latter had won from the penultimate King of Babylonia in 1160. Assyria suffered a still more serious setback with the Elamite occupation of the Assyrian towns of Arrapha (Kirkuk) and Titurru (Altun Köprü). G. C. Cameron has suggested that it was this humiliation that precipitated the fall from power and then the death of King Ashshur-dan I, old and feeble after forty-six years of rule. If this is accurate, Shilhak-Inshushinak's campaign would have taken place in 1133 B.C.

At that time, southern Babylonia was ruled by King Itti-marduk-balatu, the second ruler of the second kingdom of Isin. Spurred on by a desperate concern for his own skin, he apparently attempted to catch the Elamites on their flank, but Shilhak-Inshushinak wasted no time in embarking on yet another campaign, in which he advanced to the Tigris, overcame the Babylonians, pursued them as they fled westwards to the Euphrates, and scored yet another victory. This probably marked the end of the rule of Itti-marduk-balatu. He was replaced as King of Isin in 1130 by Ninurta-nadin-shumi, who was in his turn succeeded in 1124 by Nebuchadnezzar I, fourth ruler of the second dynasty of Isin. It is likely that Shilhak-Inshushinak died soon after in Susa, and it was under Nebuchadnezzar's rule that Babylon launched the decisive attack on Elam.

When Shilhak-Inshushinak died in about 1120, his younger brother Shimut-nika-tash was already dead, and so the throne descended to the eldest son of Queen Nahhunte-utu, who was *Hutelutush-Inshushinak* ('god Inshushinak is gracious to his deeds'). Inscriptions of his found in Susa are neither numerous nor comprehensive, and yet they are among the most revealing

133

of Elamite inscriptions because they expose with a particular clarity many peculiarities of Elamite life.

Strangely enough, Hutelutush-Inshushinak renounced the old and respected titles of his ancestors, for he no longer calls himself 'King of Anshan and Susa' but 'Expander of the kingdom, tyrant [?*menir*] of Elam and Susa.' It is possible that these phrases conceal constitutional reorganization; in any case, the texts bearing on the new king give one the uncertain feeling that the glory of his royal forbears is already somewhat tarnished.

Hutelutush-Inshushinak dedicated a new stone door-hinge to the temple of the twin gods Shimut and Manzat in Susa, although the gift was primarily intended for the goddess. The king always preferred to address his appeals to goddesses, in particular to Ishnikarab and Upurkupak. Inshushinak is summarily demoted and the other male deities, at least in the available sources, are totally ignored. The inscription on this door-hinge reads thus: 'O Goddess Manzat, great mistress! I am Hutelutush-Inshushinak, son of Kutir-nahhunte and of Shilhak-Inshushinak, expander of the kingdom. I desired my life, the life of Nahhunte-utu, my gracious mother, and the lives of my brothers and sisters, and so I had this door-hinge made of stone and brought to the temple of the goddess Manzat and of the Elamite god Simutta.'

It seems odd to modern ears that Hutelutush-Inshushinak should describe himself as the son of two fathers, not only of his real father Kutir-nahhunte but also of his father's brother Shilhak-Inshushinak. The fact that these kings both in turn took their (probable) sister Nahhunte-utu to wife was clearly seen by the son not only as an adequate justification of this dual paternity, but as a positive honour. And this was not all; in another inscription Hutelutush-Inshushinak even describes himself as the 'son' of Shutruk-nahhunte, of Kutir-nahhunte and of Shilhak-Inshushinak; in reality, these three were his grandfather, his father and his uncle. The solution to this puzzle lies in the fact, hitherto unsuspected, that Elamite possessed *two* words for 'son', with quite separate meanings and implications. This is also a testimony to the highly individual Elamite family feeling, which we are fundamentally unable to experience as they did : a distinction between male and female inheritance unknown today even to biology.

We may conclude from the inscription on the door-hinge that the king's mother Nahhunte-utu was still alive at the time of its composition. She did not figure in subsequent texts, and did not long survive her two husbands, or brothers. The inscription also proves that Hutelutush-Inshushinak was childless, because straight after his mother he mentions his brothers and sisters. These were really only his half-brothers and sisters, the children of his mother's second marriage to his uncle Shilhak-Inshushinak. In Elamite eyes this made no difference; more important was their common descent from the 'gracious mother' who now nurtured their legitimacy.

Our only information on Elam's external politics under Hutelutush-Ishushinak is to be found in reports from Nebuchadnezzar I, who was involved in desperate attempts to shatter Elamite dominance in southern Mesopotamia. In 1115 B.C. he decided with great reluctance to launch an attack on Elam.

Nebuchadnezzar's writings make it clear for what enormous stakes he was playing. 'I spoke to myself in fear, anxiety, and despair : "I will not be as my predecessor, who [?]languishes in Elam; rather will I die".' His reference to the king in exile probably means Ninurta-nadin-shumi of Isin, who had ruled from 1130 to 1125 : the last Kassite, dragged into exile by Kutir-nahhunte in 1157, could not still be alive. From this we can infer that, in the course of his victorious advance to the Euphrates, Shilhak-Inshushinak had also captured the third king of the second kingdom of Isin and then taken him back to Elam. At any rate, Nebuchadnezzar was resisting such a fate as this with all the strength he could muster.

He continues : 'I will not shun the fight with the Elamite, I will not turn back. And so I waited for him with my remaining troops at the overflow of the Uqnû (Karkheh). But Nergal, the strongest of the gods, struck my warriors [with sickness].' At this point there is a lacuna in the clay tablet; his report resumes: 'I feared death and dared not risk battle, I turned back. In the town of Kar-bur-apil-sin I sat as if bemused. The Elamite [Hutelutush-Inshushinak] came, and I fled from the town. I lay on the bed of wailing and sighing and implored the gods, weeping . . .' The rest has been broken off, but the outcome is not in doubt: Nebuchadnezzar submitted to the Elamites and abandoned all hope for himself and his kingdom of Isin.

But help arrived from an unexpected quarter. The Elamite king seems to have kept his kingdom on too tight a rein, for not only did two apparently influential priests and their god Ria call upon Nebuchadnezzar from Susiana, but also the Prince of Bit-Karziabku in the Elamite border country of Dêr betrayed his faith to Elam and turned to Babylonia. Filled with new hope, Nebuchadnezzar at once appointed Prince *Lakti-Shikhu* commander of his chariots of war, and in the year 1110 risked a renewed attack on Elam from Dêr. Details survive in a stone charter of freedom which the king granted to his ally Lakti-Shichu on his triumphant return home and which allowed him certain privileges in Bit-Karziabku. The charter runs thus:

Nebuchadnezzar, sent forth by Marduk, king of the gods, seized his weapons to avenge Akkad. From Dêr he marched twice thirty hours, in the month of Tammuz (about July) he embarked on the campaign. [The stones] of the way burnt like fire, the water gave out, the horses died of exhaustion, the legs of the men lost their power. But the noble king marched on, he did not fear the unapproachable land, he urged on the horses in the yoke. Lakti-Shikhu, Prince of Bit-Karziabku, the commander of his chariots, whose place was at his right hand, did not leave his lord in the hour of trouble, and impelled his chariots onwards. The powerful king reached the bank of the

Ulai, and the two rulers [Hutelutush-Inshushinak and Nebuchadnezzar] opened battle. In the thick of it, flames curled up, dust obscured the sunlight, and the struggle raged like a hurricane . . .

On this occasion, the fortunes of war favoured the Babylonian. 'Hutelutush-Inshushinak, King of Elam, hid himself in his mountain.' This mysterious phrase signifies that Hutelutush-Inshushinak met his death at this time. 'King Nebuchadnezzar was victorious, he overcame the land of Elam and plundered its treasures.'

Although this Babylonian domination was not to be permanent for Elam, the battle by the Ulai not far from Susa set the seal on its ensuing fate. Many centuries later, this decisive victory was still not forgotten; the Babylonian astrologers connect it in their historical reports with a meteor as the omen 'that Nebuchadnezzar decimated Elam.' The zenith was past.

It is to be presumed that *Shilhana-hamru-Lagamar*, eldest son of Shilhak-Inshushinak, came to the throne in accordance with long tradition, being the eldest (half-) brother of the vanquished Hutelutush-Inshushinak. We know nothing of his reign.

It appears that at this period, around 1110 B.C., Susa was so severely damaged that for some time it forfeited its position as the capital of Elam; at any rate, for nearly four centuries no texts survive from the city. The final years of the Shutrukids are hidden in an obscurity no less profound than that which shrouded the end of the kingdoms of Awan, Simashki and the Eparti. Elam's great classical period comes to an abrupt end, and 'the rest is silence'.

# CHAPTER VII

# The Later Kingdom
# (c. 750-640 B.C.)

After Nebuchadnezzar's victory by the Ulai, almost three hundred years elapsed before the complete textual silence was broken. This happened for the first time in 821 B.C., when the Assyrian king Shamshi-Adad V overcame an army composed of Elamites, Chaldees and Aramaics. Elam itself does not reappear until 742, when, as we learn from Babylonian Chronicles: 'King *Humban-nikash* ascended the throne in Elam.' Later Elamite sources also refer to his father *Humban-tahrah*, who would therefore probably have founded the new kingdom in the middle of the eighth century B.C.

This new kingdom of Elam lasted little more than a century. Its history was characterized by two features: the first was Elam's struggle against Assyria, newly supreme in Mesopotamia, whose ascendancy had transformed the traditional rivalry between Elam and Babylonia to a close-knit alliance; the second was the emergence of the Medes and Persians in the mountains of Iran.

The beginnings of the Arian immigration into Iran may be traced back to the period around 1000 B.C. The Medes and Persians first occupied the area that was once Gutium and is now Persian Kurdestan, south of Lake Urmia and along the military road from Babylon to Raga in Teheran. Here they were met for the first time by the Assyrian King Shalmaneser III in 835 B.C. During the early years of the seventh century, the Persians disassociated themselves from the Medes, who were of shared ancestry, and migrated to the east along the Zagros, where they occupied the area of Parsa, named after them (Persis in Greek), which now centres around Shiraz. From this base they gradually pressed forward to the east under their kings Teispes and Cyrus I from the house of Achaemenes; advancing along the military road from Persepolis to Susa they appropriated more and more of Elam's possessions in Anshan. These two developments, the recurring attacks that Elam carried out on Assyria and the gradual occupation of her eastern territories by the Persians, undermined the later Elamite kingdom to such a degree that in 640 B.C. it finally succumbed to Assurbanipal.

Hand in hand with this decline went the transformation of the ancient Elamite federal system into a body politic whose links were of the slenderest. Members of the ruling house of the Later Elamite period quarrelled so bitterly among themselves that at times the king of Susa was forgotten, and the Babylonian neighbours came to consider the Prince of Western Elam as king rather than the rightful one. As far as possible the Assyrian politicians took advantage of the resentment that festered between the royal brothers in Elam; only a few dominant characters emerge from the gloom which, from an historical point of view, surrounded the Later Elamite kingdom. Among them was its real founder, King Humban-nikash, who ruled Elam for twenty-five years, up to 717 B.C.

There are no surviving Elamite texts about him, but he is mentioned and indeed eulogized in Babylonian chronicles, which state that in 720 Humban-nikash overcame the famous Assyrian King Sargon near Dêr: 'He inflicted a crushing defeat on Assyria.' King Merodach-baladan, King of Babylonia, hastened to bring troops to the aid of the Elamites, but turned back as he arrived too late for the battle. Even this, the first

surviving text from the Late Elamite period, sets the stage for
the last acts of Elamite history, down to the final collapse :
'Elam, together with her ally Babylonia, exerted all her strength
to fight off Assyrian oppression, until in the end she was forced
to yield.'

Three years after the victory, Humban-nikash was succeeded
in 717 B.C. by the 'son of his sister', *Shutur-nahhunte*. He was
one of the most noteworthy kings that the Later Elamite kingdom produced; furthermore, he bequeathed to us a number
of inscriptions through which it is possible to sketch in the out-
lines of his character.

Shutur-nahhunte was the son of an otherwise unknown
Indada, a fact which we learn not from him but from a rock-
inscription set up by his vassal Hanne in the mountains of
Ayapir (Izeh/Malamir). Shutur-nahhunte for his own part
describes himself as the *shak* of the King *Humban-nimena*, an
assertion to which we shall return later. In his earliest inscription Shutur-nahhunte bestows on himself once more the ancient
and honourable title of 'King of Anshan and Susa', and he also
styles himself the 'expander of his kingdom'. Even from this we
can detect his ambition to preserve the splendour he had
inherited and to follow in the footsteps of his famous ancestors.

Shutur-nahhunte's yearning for fame and grandeur had one
surprising manifestation : in all subsequent inscriptions he uses
a slightly altered name – all at once, he is called Shutruk-
nahhunte. The historian finds that he must rechristen Shutur-
nahhunte *Shutruk-nahhunte II* although his contemporaries
were reluctant to adopt this change; some, indeed, ignored it
completely. His vassal Hanne in Ayapir, for one, continued to
use the old name Shutur-nahhunte, as did the Babylonians,
allies or no allies. But it was the Assyrians who first seriously
decided against humouring their opponent in Elam by recog-
nizing his new name. For this change of name was part of a
campaign to show the world that Shutruk-nahhunte II was
determined to follow in the wake of the great Shutruk-nahhunte

of the twelfth century; it amounted to a challenge to Assyrian supremacy in Mesopotamia. However, King Sargon was temporarily engaged on other concerns and quietly shelved the matter.

In one of his inscriptions, Shutruk-nahhunte II no longer refers to himself as 'King of Anshan and Susa' but as 'Expander of my kingdom, ruler of Elam, beloved servant of the gods Humban and Inshushinak'. There follows an unusually revealing remark that three once-powerful kings have united for his well-being, and this is why the throne has come to him. This remark is significant in relation to the religious and spiritual history of Elam. It seems clear that the souls of the departed were relied upon to unite in intervening in earthly events. It is also of historical interest, for of the three 'powerful kings' for whose spiritual support Shutruk-nahhunte is appealing, we have so far only met the first two, Hutelutush-Inshushinak and Shilhina-hamru-Lagamar, the two last Shutrukids. The third is a certain King Humban-nimena; Shutruk-nahhunte describes himself as his *shak* in almost all inscriptions. It goes without saying that *shak* cannot mean 'son' in this context, but simply 'male child' or 'male successor'. In all probability this Humban-nimena was the very last of the Shutrukids, perhaps a grandson of Shilhak-Inshushinak, and otherwise unknown.

It is an open question whether or not Shutruk-nahhunte II was really descended from this king, but it is important that the new rulers of Elam felt themselves to be descendants of the Shutrukids. Thus, the three and a half centuries between 1100 and 750, far from being a period of complete textual silence, were years of active and continuing transition : in exactly the same way as Shutruk-nahhunte II considered himself as the 'child' of the Shutrukids, so once the Shutrukid Hutelutush-Inshushinak and, before him, the Igehalkid Humban-numena saw themselves as the descendants of the Eparti Silhaha and of his sister. The Eparti in their turn felt themselves to be the heirs of the kings of Simashki, who probably thought that they were continuing the house of Awan. Throughout a period of two thousand years, there is evidence of an unbroken sense of historical identity, a consciousness of family loyalty, which is truly astonishing.

Unfortunately the second half of Shutruk-nahhunte's inscription, in which he alludes to the 'three powerful kings', still for the most part defies elucidation. It is however clear that the king, with the help of his god Inshushinak, had overcome the town of Karindash; Shutruk-nahhunte II, like his great namesake, must have advanced as far as modern Kerend on the military road from Babylon to Raga. It was probably on this same campaign that he led his army right across Luristan, past Khurramabad (once probably Simashki), Nehawand and Harsin, right out through Kermanshah. It seems likely that it is this very 'expansion of the kingdom' that is described on a victory stele of Shutruk-nahhunte II; the inscription occupies more than eighty lines and is largely untranslatable. The king tells us in it that he has overcome thirty-two territories in all. Of the vast number of place names only one can so far be mapped with any certainty : the land of Arman, which Shutruk-nahhunte II claims to have captured, is now modern Hulwan (or Sarpol). The Elamite troops would therefore have advanced further from Karindash/Kerend, over the pass of Paytaq, and down on to the edge of the Mesopotamian plain.

Whenever he overcame a city, Shutruk-nahhunte II used to send out his high priest Shutruru to collect sacrificial cattle as tribute and to set up statues of the Elamite king. As a sign of gratitude for the help the gods had given him in achieving these victories, Shutruk-nahhunte dedicated the aforesaid stele in Susa to the Temple of Inshushinak, and on the same day that it was put up, the 25th of the month of Lanlube (about the middle of October – the year is unfortunately omitted) he ordained a daily sacrifice of one wether for the priest of the temple, two wethers for the high priest, and in addition a bushel of flour for the witnesses. Nor did the king forget the goddesses Lagamar and Pinikir; he threatened any man that harmed the stele and the accompanying dedication with the curse of the sun-god Nahhunte, who would make his name 'wither'.

In the shadow of Shutruk-nahhunte's acquisitive policy, his vassal Hanne, son of Tahhihi, was building up his own small kingdom in the eastern mountain province of Ayapir. His court was closely modelled on the palace at Susa. Prince Hanne has made a deeper impression on posterity than he really deserved, simply because he, or his apparently highly efficient minister, hit upon the happy idea of having monuments chiselled into the rock-faces and grottos on either side of the valley of Izeh. These included not only large numbers of reliefs, but also three extended inscriptions in Elamite, of which two have been preserved in almost perfect condition. One of these inscribed reliefs in the gorge of Kul-e Farah (Plates 14 and 15) shows Prince Hanne moving to the right, with his hands crossed at his girdle in prayer. Although the head is mutilated, a round cap is still visible, from which his hair streams out in a long plait. His chin is concealed by a long curling beard. His full robe, caught in by a broad girdle, is patterned with horizontal stripes and reaches down to his bare feet. Over it, the prince is wearing a long cloak, fringed and bordered with rosettes; a sartorial invention, it appears, of the Elamites.

The upper of the two smaller figures behind Hanne represents his minister Shutruru (not to be confused with his namesake the high priest of Shutruk-nahhunte II); the lower depicts his cup-bearer. The minister, who is clearly also Hanne's general, is clad in a robe that is no more than knee-length; on his back he had a quiver and on his left arm a bow. Before these three figures a religious ceremony is being conducted, as we have described in Chapter II. To a musical accompaniment, a priest is pouring out the blood of three rams at the altar, while assistants drag up a humped cow and a mountain goat as further sacrifices.

The twenty-four lines of the inscription are an appeal to the gods Tirutir, Napir and Shimut. He has put up his carving under the powerful magic protection (*kiten*) of the god Humban. The gods Tirutir and Napir had furthered his rise, and so, by their favour, he has subdued a large area and brought back a quantity of plunder. But he did not betray the faith he owed to King Shutruk-nahhunte as his vassal (Hanne still refers to him as Shutur-nahhunte). He successfully subdued two uprisings, one at Shilhite, the other on the river Pirrin, which we assume to be the river Karun. 'He who harms my carving, who inserts his name as possessor, who hammers it away, who appropriates it,' runs the end of the inscription, 'may he lose the healing of the goddess Niarsina (Venus), may he be deprived of and expelled from her favour, may he be undone! As one lost on the earth may he walk no more under the sun.'

On the other side of the valley of Izeh, Hanne had two life-size reliefs installed above the grotto of Shekaf-e Salman. The lefthand one (Plate 18) shows him with his wife, the *Princess Ammatena*, and with their son. He explicitly says that this relief was inspired by his minister Shutruru, and, as a sign of gratitude, Hanne has had the minister and his family – in all two men, one woman and two children – immortalized on the righthand end of the same rock-face. It is unfortunate that the Elamite inscription above it has been almost completely destroyed.

However, another inscription, thirty-six lines long, has been preserved in almost perfect condition inside the cave, with its spring. In it Hanne tells us that in the sight of Parti he has put a magical protection on his own inscription, on his child's, and on Huhin's (his 'beloved Sister-wife'). This claim will not tally with the words on the robe worn by the woman at the top left of the rock, which identify her as the Lady Ammatena. If we are dealing with one and the same princess, *Ammatena* could perhaps be intended as a title, meaning 'gracious mother'. But equally, if we have to deal with two different wives, the description of the princess Huhin as wife and sister remains important: even provincial rulers followed the 'family custom' of the Elamite kings in marrying their sisters.

The cave and inscription appear to have been sacred to Parti, the mother-goddess of Anshan: the inscription specifically mentions a temple dedicated to her. 'A learned man who reads my carving while praying,' remarks Hanne towards the end of the inscription, 'who praises the construction, may his wish be granted.' But the destroyer of the monument shall be smitten to the ends of the earth by the sceptre of the god Humban, of the goddess Kiririsha (who now reappears alongside Parti, mother of the gods) and of the god Tirutir ('who made earth and water'). 'May he forfeit the blessing of Parti. May his generation be cut off under the moon and sun. May he have no descendants.'

Let us now leave Hanne and return to Shutruk-nahhunte II, his overlord in Susa, where we find that an important part of world history is taking place.

In the year 710 B.C., King *Sargon* of Assyria had marched into battle against Babylonia. King *Merodach-baladan* was forced to a rapid and nocturnal flight: 'Merodach-baladan had ruled over Babylon for twelve years. Now Sargon ascended its throne. Merodach-baladan, at the head of his great ones, fled to Elam.' So much for the Babylonian chronicle, terse and to the point as ever. The enemy is much more communicative; Sargon the Assyrian tells us maliciously that Merodach-baladan had 'sent the following to Shutur-nahhunte the Elamite (of course, Sargon does not call him Shutruk-nahhunte!) hoping that he will avenge him: his royal insignia, his bed, his throne, his footstool, his royal water-jar and even his chain. And indeed the evil Elamite accepted his presents, but was afraid of My Weapons, barred his way, and forbade him to go further.' Whereupon Merodach-baladan fell into sorrow and despair. In fact Shutruk-nahhunte did grant asylum in Elam to his sworn ally in the expectation of a later joint campaign against Mesopotamia.

They saw their opportunity when Sargon died five years later in 705 and his son *Sennacherib* ascended the throne in Assyria. In 1703 Merodach-baladan set out for central Babylonia at the head of a strong supporting force of Elamite troops, consisting of bowmen and cavalry; he was accompanied by two generals and ten staff-officers belonging to Shutruk-nahhunte. The Babylonians rallied with enthusiasm; the Aramaic tribes of the Tigris joined him; and at Kish he joined battle with the Assyrian troops, who were beaten by the united strength of the Babylonians and the Elamites.

It was not until King Sennacherib himself marched into Kish that their good fortune changed. Merodach-baladan lost his nerve and fled into the swampy plains of southern Mesopotamia, abandoning his Elamite allies to their fate. The victorious Sennacherib occupied Babylon, but was not able to recapture the fugitive Merodach-baladan.

Meanwhile, the Elamite and Babylonian declaration of hostilities was not without effect in the Mediterranean lands. Sennacherib had swooped down on Tyre and Sidon, at which point *Hezekiah*, King of Judah, counting on Egypt's support, also joined the alliance against him: even he did not dare assert himself unaided against the Assyrian king. In 701 B.C. Sennacherib besieged Jerusalem, and did not withdraw his troops until Hezekiah had paid over a tribute of thirty talents of gold and three hundred talents of silver. He subsequently became sick to death, as we read in Isaiah 38, but recovered.

News of Hezekiah's illness and subsequent recovery found its way to Merodach-baladan, who was now exiled in Elam; he took note of the fact that Sennacherib had failed to capture Jerusalem and had been forced to content himself with Hezekiah's tribute. In an attempt to extend the Elamite-Babylonian alliance, Merodach-baladan sent his chancellors on a mission to the King of Judah in 700; these ambassadors were to congratulate Hezekiah on his recovery and try to persuade him to join the alliance against Assyria. We have a remarkable account of this in Kings II, 20:12–19.

And in Isaiah 39 we read :

And Hezekiah was glad of them, and shewed them the house of his precious things, the silver and the gold, and the spices, and the precious ointment, and all the house of his armour, and all that was found in his treasures; there was nothing in his house, nor in all his dominion, that Hezekiah shewed them not. Then came Isaiah the prophet unto King Hezekiah, and said to him : What said these men? And from whence came they unto thee? And Hezekiah said : They are come from a far country unto me, even from Babylon. Then said he : What have they seen in thy house? And Hezekiah said : All that is in mine house have they seen; there is nothing among my treasures that I have not shewed them. Then said Isaiah unto Hezekiah : Hear the word of the Lord of Hosts : Behold, thy day is come, that all that is in thine house, and that which thy fathers have laid up in store until this day, shall be carried to Babylon : nothing shall be left, saith the Lord. And of thy sons which shall issue from thee, which thou shalt beget, shall they take away; and they shall be eunuchs in the palace of the King of Babylon.

King Hezekiah was not unduly disturbed by Isaiah's prophecy, which was fulfilled a hundred years later when Nebuchadnezzar II (597 B.C.) led Jehoiachin, King of Judah, to Babylon in captivity, and stole all the Jerusalem treasure. The sources tell us nothing of the ambassadors' return to their lord on the Elamite coast of the Persian Gulf. The following year, 699, Sennacherib installed his own son as king of Babylonia, and at the same time a palace revolution took place in Elam. Shutruk-nahhunte II was incarcerated by his younger brother *Hallushu-Inshushinak*, who then usurped his place as King in Susa.

In the only inscription that survives from his reign, Hallushu-Inshushinak refers to himself as a *shak* of King Humban-tahrah. This is another instance of the Elamite word meaning not 'son' but simply a 'male descendant': Humban-tahrah was in fact Hallushu-Inshushinak's great-uncle. In the same inscription, the new king refers to himself unashamedly as the 'expander of the kingdom'. He prays thus to god Inshushinak, to whom he had dedicated a temple of glazed brick: 'Do not consider my victory as troublesome.'

For five years all went well. Merodach-baladan had established himself in the Elamite coastal town of Nagitu on the Persian Gulf; but in 694 B.C., the Assyrian King Sennacherib renewed his aggression. Phoenician ship-builders were co-opted to construct a fleet of ships on the Tigris and the Euphrates, but, as the lower reaches of the Tigris were still in Elamite hands, the ships were forced to halt their advance half-way to the Persian Gulf. They were then dragged up on to dry land, and transferred on rollers to the Arahtu canal, continuing along it till they reached the Euphrates, where the Assyrian troops went on board. King Sennacherib, however, left the fleet to sail on alone to the Persian Gulf and opted for the safer land route. After a delay of five days, caused by unfavourable winds and high seas, the fleet crossed the Gulf and rejoined Sennacherib's land forces on the Elamite coast. Despite furious and unremitting resistance, one Elamite coastal town after another fell under Assyrian sway; Sennacherib divided the captive Elamites and exiled Babylonians among his soldiers 'like sheep'. It seems that Merodach-baladan was by now already dead.

In reply to the Assyrian incursions into the 'sea-lands', the Elamite king staged a manoeuvre no less bold than cunning. As early as October 694, Hallushu-Inshushinak overcame Sippar in the north of Babylonia, thus cutting the Assyrian line of communications. Sennacherib's son was captured in Babylonia and dragged off to Elam, and in his place, Hallushu-Inshushinak set the Babylonian Nergal-ushezib on the throne. However, his rule was fated to be short. Once more, Sennacherib proved that he had the upper hand: at the end of September 693 he overcame the allied Elamite and Babylonian forces at Nippur in central Babylonia; Nergal-ushezib was taken captive to

Assyria. The vanquished Hallushu-Inshushinak made his way back to Susa, but when in mid-October 693 he reached the capital, 'the people of Susa', according to Babylonian chronicles, 'shut the gate before him and slew him.' In his place, his eldest son *Kudur-nahhunte* became king.

Sennacherib was right when he saw the violent reversal of power at Susa as a sign of internal weakness in Elam. Still in the winter of 693, he launched a campaign against Kudur-nahhunte, who fled from the Assyrians to Hidali 'in the far mountains', which was probably near modern Behbehan on the road from Susa to Persepolis. It was only frost, heavy snow, and high water on the Karkheh that forced Sennacherib to turn back in January 692, and in spite of this Kudur-nahhunte was unable to hold out, and at the end of July of the same year, we learn from the Babylonian chronicles that 'Kudur, King of Elam was captured and killed during an uprising.'

The violent overthrow of three successive kings of the same house: such a thing had never before happened in Elam. There could be no clearer sign of the collapse of the kingdom. The slain king was followed by his younger brother *Humban-nimena.*

The events of the next year, 691, are fully reported by Sennacherib:

In my eighth campaign I ordered a march on Babylon. When the Babylonians had word of this, they were much afraid. They opened the treasury of Esangila (the temple of Marduk in Babylon), took from it much gold and silver and jewels, and sent it to Humban-nimena, King of Elam, with the message: 'Come to Babylon to our aid! Help us!' But he, the King of Elam, a fool without sense or understanding, accepted the gifts.'

The rest is partially mutilated, but makes it clear that Humban-nimena called out his army.

Among the Elamite troops, there were also warriors 'from Parsuash'. This is the first appearance in Elamite history of this obscure name, 'land of the Persians', no longer the area to the south of Lake Urmia, but part of Anshan. It seems that the Persians had not been there very long at this time (691). Their king was probably called *Achaemenes* (*Hakhamanish*), and was the founder of the house of the Achaemenids from which the world conquerors Cyrus and Darius were later to come. Achaemenes, founder of the dynasty, was followed in about 675 by his son Teispes or Chaish-pish. This Persian immigration was the first time that Elam had been threatened from the east. Although the kings of Elam and their vassals in Anshan were able to keep these upstarts under their control, the Persian threat nevertheless became ever more serious; the participation of Persian troops in the military advance that King Humban-nimena led into Mesopotamia probably had to be bought with Babylonian gold.

In addition to the Babylonians and the Persians, the king had enlisted the support of other allies, among them the Ellipi in the north of Luristan and the Aramaic tribes from the Tigris. 'All these moved determinedly in, together with the King of Babylon, and flung themselves upon me,' wrote Sennacherib. The battle took place on the Tigris, on the plain of Halule, near what is now Samarra. The Assyrian king boasts of an overwhelming victory: 'Humban-untash, general to the King of Elam, a brave man, the commander of his troops and his chief support, and also his best soldiers, who wear golden daggers and heavy rings of shining gold on their wrists – these I quickly overthrew and vanquished.' Finally, Sennacherib gives us a vivid picture of how he dealt with them: 'But Humban-nimena, the King of Elam, and Mushezib-Marduk, the King of Babylon, both abandoned their tents and, to save their own lives, drove over the bodies of their fallen troops.' He says that he had the two fugitives pursued with war-chariots and cavalry. Sennacherib concludes this verbose and somewhat overdone account with the claim: 'But when I saw that the two had [out of fear] defecated into their chariots, I let them go and spared their lives . . .'

The explanation provided by their opponents is quite at variance: according to Babylonian chronicles it was rather that Humban-nimena overcame the Assyrian. In reality the outcome of the battle of Halule was probably indecisive; in any case, Sennacherib failed in this attempt of 691 to destroy the Elamite-Babylonian alliance, and Mushezib-Marduk remained King of Babylon.

But Sennacherib had luck on his side. At the beginning of April 689, Humban-nimena had a stroke: 'His mouth became stiff, so that he could no longer speak,' says the Babylonian chronicle, and the King of Assyria was not slow to seize his opportunity. He descended on Babylonia; in December 689 he captured the capital, Babylon, and took Mushezib-Marduk captive to Nineveh. Two months later, at the end of February 688, Humban-nimena died in Susa.

His heir was *Humban-haltash I*, probably one of his cousins; but we have no Elamite information about him. His reign appears to have been a peaceful one until his death in 681, which is described by the Babylonians: 'On the 23rd of Teshrit (roughly mid-October 681) King Humban-haltash was smitten by a sudden illness in the early afternoon; he died at sunset that same evening.'

It seems that yet another cousin of the three preceding rulers was still alive in the capital, namely *Shilhak-Inshushinak II*, son of Ummanunu, and he probably came to the throne. A bronze model commissioned by him has been found in Susa; he dedicated it to the temple of the goddess Venus, or Niarsina. The Mesopotamian sources do not even recognize him; in their eyes one of his nephews, *Humban-haltash II*, who may have been the son of Kudar-nahhunte, became King of Elam in 681.

Humban-haltash II attempted to restore relations with Assyria. In the same year (681) Sennacherib had been assassinated by his son, *Asarhaddon*, who then seized power. Six years later, in 675, Humban-haltash embarked on a campaign of pillage and murder against the Babylonian town of Sippar;

but at the end of September of the same year, he 'died in his palace without having been ill.' He was succeeded by his brother *Urtaki*. As there is so far no record of him in Elamite sources, we do not know exactly what he was called – perhaps Ur-tak-Inshushinak. Like his brother before him, Urtaki tried to establish reasonable relationships with Assyria, but when Asarhaddon died in 668, to be succeeded by his son Assurbanipal, Urtaki seems to have changed his policy. This may have some connection with the fact that Shilhak-Inshushinak II, that shadowy ruler, was relieved of his duties in Susa by his son *Tempt-Humban-Inshushinak*.

The appearance of Tempt-Humban-Inshushinak at once restored Elam to its former glory. He succeeded gradually in usurping his cousin Urtaki, and in assuming overall supremacy. Five of his inscriptions have survived in Susa, but unfortunately they are both partly mutilated and – as usual – incomprehensible. Most of the relevant information is to be found in the inscriptions of his vindictive opponent, Assurbanipal; in his eyes, Te-Umman (the Assyrian spelling of Tempt-Humban-Inshushinak) was the 'arch-fiend'.

Urtaki's alliance with Tempt-Humban-Inshushinak seems to have given him the courage for an attack on Mesopotamia in 665, when Assurbanipal was engaged on campaigns in Egypt and Ethiopia. For this, the Assyrian king reproached him bitterly as having forgotten the favours which his father Asarhaddon granted him, and having shown ingratitude where he himself was concerned:

> When hard times came upon Elam and famine filled the land, I sent him [Urtaki] corn to keep his people alive. I was his support. Those of his people who had fled from the hard times, and had found refuge in Assyria till rain fell once more and there was a harvest – I sent these people, who had kept themselves alive in my country, back to him. In my heart I should never have expected an attack from the Elamite, never have suspected him of hatred.

News of this attack by Urtaki reached Assurbanipal in Nineveh, his capital. 'I was undecided in my mind; for his best soldiers, who were for peace, constantly sent letters to me. In order to learn more about the King of Elam, I sent a scout out in haste, and he went and returned and reported with authority : the Elamites have overrun all Akkad like a swarm of locusts and are proceeding towards Babylon.' So Assurbanipal mobilized his army. According to his report, Urtaki then turned back to Elam; 'I pursued him to the boundaries of his country.' And once again, a King of Assyria was spared considerable inconvenience by the sudden death of his enemy.

And for Tempt-Humban-Inshushinak also, this was the moment he had been waiting for. This son of Shilhak-Inshushinak seems to have had his eye on the sole supremacy for some time, and now that both his cousins were dead, he took the plunge. Flying in the face of all Elamite traditions of family loyalty, he attempted to take into custody the descendants and relations of his two predecessors Humban-haltash II and Urtaki. Faced with his intrigues, the two sons of the former and the three sons of the latter fled to Assurbanipal for protection; in all sixty Elamite princes and princesses came together in Nineveh, along with a large posse of archers. 'They fled to me before the murderous rage of their uncle Te-Umman, and seized my royal feet,' wrote the Assyrian king. Thereupon, Tempt-Humban-Inshushinak sent Humban-tahrah and the eunuch Nabu-damiq as ambassadors to Assurbanipal, demanding the return of his gaggle of nephews, but Assurbanipal waved the 'shameless messengers' back and granted asylum to the Elamite princes.

Since Assurbanipal was much occupied in the ensuing years with Syria, Asia Minor and north-west Iran, Tempt-Humban-Inshushinak was able to establish his supremacy undisturbed. In his inscriptions he boasts of great victories over the 'land of the wicked' and over the people of Lallarip. It is conceivable that these 'wicked' people were the Persians in Anshan; the Lallarips could be found in northern Luristan. He exacted a crippling tribute from both races. To show his thanks, he then dedicated a temple of baked brick to the goddess Pinikir in Susa, and he also made known the help that Humban and Inshushinak granted him during these manoeuvres.

A general view of the king's inscriptions leaves us with the erroneous impression that Elam had regained its previous footing under his administration: in reality its downfall was imminent. Alas, all reports on the subsequent fate of Tempt-Humban-Inshushinak emanate from his arch-enemy Assurbanipal, in whose eyes 'Te-Umman' was indeed the 'arch-fiend'. Although the accounts provided by the Assyrian king must be rated as exaggerated and sometimes distorted, these faults are amply compensated for by his lucidity. Assurbanipal also had the break with Elam permanently recorded on stone reliefs in his palace at Nineveh, with inscribed clay tablets to explain the pictures. Taken all in all, these form sources of rare vividness.

'Te-Umman thought evil,' wrote Assurbanipal, 'but the moon-god was planning misfortune for him.' This refers to an eclipse of the moon on 13 July 653 B.C., when Urtaki had already been dead for ten years and by which time Tempt-Humban-Inshushinak had ruled Elam in peace for ten years. Assurbanipal positively revels in his account of how the evil omen sent by the moon-god affected his enemy: 'At that time, a sickness came upon Te-Umman: his lips were paralysed, his eyes turned in his face and looked towards the middle of his face.'

However, Assurbanipal had to concede that Tempt-Humban-Inshushinak was not deterred by this fit – apparently epileptic – from mobilizing the Elamite army. 'In the month of Ab [August 653] while I remained in Arbela (Erbil), news was brought to me of the approach of the Elamite.' The Assyrian king appears to have been in some trouble at this time, and his anxiety was only allayed by a favourable vision that appeared to his seer. In September 653 he had the Assyrian army mobilized, and it advanced over the famous pass at Dêr into Elamite territory. Assurbanipal himself remained at home.

In the face of the advancing and usually victorious Assyrian troops, Tempt-Humban-Inshushinak withdrew to Susa, to his fortress in the Posht-e-kuh mountains. 'To save his life, he distributed gold and silver among the people of his land,' writes Assurbanipal. 'He entrenched himself opposite me on the river Ulai.' The battle was a decisive victory for the Assyrians, a blow from which the Later Elamite kingdom never recovered. Although Susa itself was not taken, Elamite losses were high. One relief from Nineveh, pieced together out of fragments (Figure 33) represents Susa, the capital, and its ziggurat, enclosed by the two arms of the Ulai. A dead Elamite and a quiver are floating in the river, and on the left, the officials of Susa gaze anxiously from the ramparts of the gate to see how the battle is proceeding.

When Tempt-Humban-Inshushinak saw that the battle was lost, he tore at his beard in desperation and then took flight.

*Figure 33*

Accompanied by his eldest son *Tamritu*, he sought refuge in a nearby palm-grove, but here the cross-pole of his chariot broke and the chariot fell upon the king. In his distress he called to his son 'Shoot thou with thy bow!' Tamritu tore his clothes in his sorrow and called to his father: 'Hold on, do not let go!' The son helped his father to rise, but the pursuers were already upon them, and Tamritu was mortally wounded by a blow from a club, while Tempt-Humban-Inshushinak was struck by an arrow. An Assyrian soldier cut off his head and bore it away by the hair in the flush of victory. 'The warriors of my battle brought the head of Te-Umman to me in haste, and in front of the gate of Assur at Nineveh threw it before my wheels,' Assurbanipal continues. 'I cut the sinews of his face with daggers and spat upon him.' Once again, the two Elamite ambassadors who had previously demanded the return of the fugitive nephews from Assurbanipal found themselves in the custody of the Assyrians:

Nabu-damiq and Humban-tahrah, the high officials whom Te-Umman had sent with an insolent message and whom I had rejected in my anger at their lord, they now beheld before me the head of their lord Te-Umman, which had been brought to me. They were filled with despair. Humban-tahrah tore at his beard, and Nabu-damiq stabbed himself with an iron dagger. But I, Assurbanipal, King of Assyria, returned joyfully to Nineveh with the head of Te-Umman, and set it up in the public gaze opposite the gate at the centre of the city.

In Elam, the Assyrian generals, acting on orders from Assurbanipal, had declared a new king, *Humban-nikash II*, the eldest of the three sons of Urtaki, who had sought asylum in Nineveh in 663. Assurbanipal established the third of these three brothers, *Tammaritu I*, as ruler of Hidali (Behbehan). But the throne of Susa went to *Atta-hamiti-Inshushinak* ('Inshushinak is a faithful father'), the son of Hutran-tempt and probably a cousin to Tempt-Humban-Inshushinak, now so shamefully slain.

During the next five years of his reign he stood aside from the centre of political activity and kept an unobtrusive watch on the confusion that was then resolving itself in Mesopotamia, in the hope that the outcome would be to Elam's advantage. It was a vain hope. Atta-hamiti-Inshushinak was almost the last of the legitimate kings of Elam and the last to be recorded in its own texts. His name only occurs once in the Assyrian texts, where it is abbreviated to Attameti.

Atta-hamiti-Inshushinak tells us on an inscribed stele that he has had this stele set up because he loved Susa and its inhabitants. It shows his head in profile (Plate 32). Of the large inscription, only incoherent fragments have survived, but even these suggest that Atta-hamiti-Inshushinak had relied principally on the mountains around Izeh/Malamir for support, because he refers to the god Ruhurater, native to this area, as his own. However, he does also appeal to Humban and Inshushinak in this inscription.

When he died in Susa in 648, he was succeeded by his son, *Humban-haltash III*, and the curtain went up on the last scene of Elam's history as an independent state. Elamite sources never refer to him, and he possessed neither the time nor the power to dedicate temples and sacred inscriptions.

In the course of two campaigns, probably in 647 and 646, Assyria overcame Elam. I do not intend to go into the details here, but during the second attack, Humban-haltash III had moved to Dur-Untash and set up a defensive position on the far (the lefthand) bank of the Diz. With enormous difficulty the Assyrians managed to cross the river and Humban-haltash fled to the mountains. This defeat involved more than the loss of all Susiana to enemy hands; it also brought with it a far-reaching Assyrian advance into Anshan up to Hidali and Bashim, as far as modern Behbehan and further to the east along the military road from Susa to Persepolis. This advance had an important consequence: the Persian king was at that time Cyrus (Kurush) I, who had but recently succeeded his father Teispes and who was the grandfather of Cyrus the Great. He came before the Assyrian generals, affirmed his loyalty to Assurbanipal, and, to prove it, sent his eldest son Aryuka as a hostage to the court at Nineveh. The Persians had no desire to delay Elam's collapse, which would bring them nothing but profit.

Terrible destruction was wrought by the Assyrians. In the late autumn of 646, the capital itself, which had until then escaped attack, fell. Assurbanipal's account of the capture of Susa has already appeared in Chapter III in connection with Elamite religion. The use of the first person in his account does not imply that he himself actually took part in the campaigns against Elam, in spite of which he writes: 'On my return from Anshan I overcame Susa, the great and sacred city, the seat of the gods of my enemies. I occupied their palaces and remained there in comfort.' This does sound as though Assurbanipal was in Susa at any rate after the victory. 'I opened their treasure-houses, where there were piles of silver and gold, of treasures and riches which had been amassed by earlier kings of Elam right up to the most recent; apart from me, no other conqueror had laid hand upon them.' The conqueror gives us a detailed catalogue of the treasures and of his vast plunder, which consisted of garments, ornaments, royal insignia, weapons, 'and all the palace furniture on which the king sat or lay, the bowls which he used for meals, washing and anointing, the chariots of triumph and of war decorated with gold and electron, the horses and mules with their gold and silver trappings – all this I took back to Assyria.'

In conclusion Assurbanipal tells us how he had the temples and sacred groves of Susa destroyed, and the graves of the Elamite kings violated:

In the course of a march which lasted fifty-five days, I transformed the land into a wilderness. I scattered salt and thistles on its meadows. The wives and daughters of the kings of Elam, of old and new family, the town governors, the commanders, the whole corps of officers including the engineers, all the inhabitants, whether male or female, old or young, the horses, the mules, the donkeys, the cattle both large and small, more numerous than a swarm of locusts – all these I dragged back to Assyria.

When the conqueror had departed, a graveyard stillness reigned over the scorched land. According to the Bible, Assurbanipal moved 'the Susanchites and the Elamites' to Samaria in Palestine (Ezra 4 :9–10). Susa became desolate. 'The screech-owl cried in the square,' we read in one chronicle. King Humban-haltash III attempted to establish himself in the mountains to the north of Susa, selecting the ruined town of Madaktu as his capital. In an attempt to ingratiate himself with Assurbanipal, he offered to surrender to him a son of that same Merodach-baladan who had once been King of Babylonia; but when Assyrian ambassadors under Bel-ibni came to Elam in 645, to collect this offering, the distraught Babylonian ordered his own shield-bearer to slay him. The Assyrian general packed the body in salt and sent it to his master in Nineveh.

But in spite of his submission, Humban-haltash III had played the game out to the end. He was forced by internal unrest to flee to north Luristan, where he was captured by the native warriors of the Ellipi and handed over to Assurbanipal, most likely in 644. Once in Nineveh, he, his cousin Tammaritu II and other captive rulers were forced to draw the triumphal car of the Assyrian king to the temple of the goddess Ishtar, where Assurbanipal inaugurated the New Year celebrations. We have no more information on the subsequent fate of this, the last king of Elam.

Elam's position remained much the same when the power of Assyria was abruptly curtailed on the death of Assurbanipal in 629. During this period the Medes, active round what is now known as Persian Kurdestan, but was then Gutium, had risen to a position of influence. Once the threat from the Scythians had been eliminated, Kyaxares (Khwakhshtra), King of the Medes, had formed an alliance with King Nabopolassar of Babylonia to encompass the conquest of Nineveh in the summer of 612. Assyria was divided up between the allies, and Susiana was allotted to Babylonia. It is true that the mountains of Anshan on the eastern border remained in Persian hands, but they were now the subjects of the Medes. It was not until Cyrus II the Great, King of Persia, had shaken off the Mede supremacy (550), and in 539 overcame Babylonia, that Susiana also became one of his acquisitions, thus bringing the whole of Elam under Persian rule.

However, in the Achaemenid empire which resulted from these victories, Elam still had an important role to play in her capacity as the third of the other two satrapies, Persia and Media. Later, in 522, when Darius inherited the power in the federation built up by Cyrus, Elam made a weak attempt at rebellion, but a delegate sent by Darius was enough to suppress it. A second and final attempt in 519 was equally abortive: in it a certain *Attameta* – a second Atta-hamiti-Inshushinak – had had himself proclaimed King of Elam. However, he was beaten in open combat by Darius's military commanders, taken as a prisoner to the great Persian king, and then executed.

This marked Elam's eventual incorporation as an integral part of the Persian empire, and from now on her history is inextricably entwined with that of Iran. One final echo survives into the period after Alexander, when, among the Seleukids and Parthians, Elymais – what one might call Elam Minor – once more had an independent existence. Because the Achaemenids kept their royal treasure at Susa, the Satraps of Huzha were also 'masters of the treasure' (*kabnishkir* in Elamite). After the downfall of the Achaemenid empire in 330 B.C., one of these 'masters of the treasure' quietly formed a small new ruling house, and this dynasty of the Kabnishkirids of Elymais survived in the area around Susa, Izeh/Malamir, and

Behbehan until the end of the second century A.D.; it remained apart from world history, stubbornly conservative, with a thin veneer of Hellenistic culture over the ancient assumptions of Elamite life. The Arabian geographers of the tenth century can offer us no more than a variation of the age-old theme of the 'wicked Elamites'.

# CHAPTER VIII

## *Art and Culture*

When, at the turn of the century, French archaeologists hit
upon well-preserved vases, bowls and goblets of painted faience
in the very bottom layer (once called Susa 1, now known as
Susa *A*), they could hardly contain their delight and astonish-
ment. Nor was it misplaced, for the pottery of Susa (Plates
20 and 26) is among the most developed that was produced by
the craftsmen of the Near East during the fourth millennium
B.C. You only have to hold one of these fragments in your hand,
to feel its thin and delicately washed surface, and to examine
the warm colours of the paint – reddish-brown, dark purple,
or blue-black – to sympathize with the delight of its discoverers.

Of course, the impression that this art-form suddenly came
into being, while natural enough seeing that the vessels derive
from the earliest occupation of Susa, is nonetheless mistaken.
American excavations in Choga Mish to the east of Susa have
proved that the Susa pottery was the outcome of centuries of
intelligent development – an obvious conclusion on *a priori*
grounds· The particular and unvarying characteristics of
this pottery consist in more than the stuff and form of the
vessels; they include especially the figured ornamentation. The
craftsmen who made these vases displayed a talent which,
after more than five thousand years, still appeals to us today :
it is the ability to represent something simultaneously both in

the concrete *and* in the abstract. There are figures of animals portrayed on these vases which combine a most vivid and life-like treatment with complete stylization. The Elamites succeeded in uniting, in the most astonishing way, what was basically irreconcilable – an ability that art historians will recognize in totally different circumstances, in the great mosques of Isfahan which the Persian masters created in the seventeenth century A.D. These buildings combine a monumental scale with the most delicate and sensitive decoration, a tiled mosaic filigree covering the vast expanse of the walls, in an apparently effortless conjunction of incompatibles. It is as though an echo of the ancient Elamite heritage were sounding across the centuries.

A celebrated example of the pottery of Susa *A* is the goblet, now in the Louvre, reproduced in Figure 34 and Plate 26. Here I quote Edith Porada's excellent description of this fourth millennium Elamite masterpiece* :

The central figure is a mountain goat, whose body is formed of two linked triangles with concave sides. The curve of its back is continued in the beautiful sweep of the horns; these form a frame for an unidentifiable round object which has a row of lines at the centre and criss-cross sections on either side. This motif may only be intended to fill the empty space, or it may be a compressed symbolic representation of a plant in a meadow. The goats – one on each side – are surrounded by a frame that tapers towards the base and thus accentuates the shape of the vessel itself. Above the frame is a row of deer-hounds, whose outstretched bodies emphasize once more the curve of the goblet, as do the dark bands that accompany each horizontal line at top and bottom. The upper edge is decorated with birds with elongated necks, which compose a very light and delicate pattern; at the base, a thick band of black provides a firm foundation. However, this description does no more than mention the component parts of the

* *Alt-Iran*, Baden-Baden, 1962, 21/22

decoration on the vessel, and cannot hope to convey the extraordinary feeling for formal balance that is revealed in every detail.

The artistic achievements of the Elamites in the third millennium have been preserved for the greater part in the work of the seal-makers. They perfected the skills that the masters of the fourth millennium had bequeathed to them. We have already mentioned in passing, at the end of Chapter I, the universally lively imagination evinced by these early Elamites; a peculiarly Elamite tendency to brood on spiritual profundities, an irresistible attraction to the darker side of nature. For preference, they portrayed imaginary hybrids and bizarre monsters. One of these hybrids is the gryphon (Figure 35), a winged lion with the head and taloned forefeet of a bird of prey. The gryphon is an original Elamite invention, and, while remaining unknown in Mesopotamia, was adopted as a symbol in Egypt. But while the Elamite shuddered to look at this strange creature, the child of his fantasy, he could not but take pleasure in it. Thus, one essential characteristic of the early Elamite was a grotesque humour of a type first affected in the West by the Mannerist school. One example of this taste for the weird is the seal in Figure 36 : monsters with tails, half monkeys, half lionesses, are sailing placidly down the river between reed-beds, the rudder to hand in the boat, escorted by large and courteous fish.

The naively naturalistic approach to artistic themes prevalent in the fourth millennium was replaced in the third by pronouncements on the powers that governed natural and political phenomena. An example of this attitude is shown in Figure 37 : a never-ending repetition of two motifs. In one of them a rampant bull is flanked by two seated lions, and in the other a standing lion is controlling two bulls who are rearing away. Pierre Amiet sees in this the abstract representation of the balance of world events; one thinks perhaps of summer and winter, succeeding each other in eternal alternation and

*Figure 34*

*Figure 35*

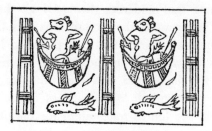

*Figure 36*

*Figure 37*

*Figure 38*

represented by the two different animals. But while this is all mere conjecture, the indisputable fact remains that we are impressed by the dramatic equilibrium of opposing forces and that we feel what extraordinary people the Elamites were·

This impression is strengthened when we examine the most remarkable example of the Elamite miniaturists' art, reproduced here in Figure 38. It is difficult to tear our eyes away from these strange figures; intrigued by their mysterious nature and behaviour, we shake our heads in puzzlement over the possible meaning that underlies them. Of all the figures that appear in the two rows of the picture, it is only the motif of a deity seated upon an animal that is depicted in Mesopotamia; all the rest is the natural product of the Elamite spirit and imagination : the half-moon and star, the scorpion with a human head, the man-bull hybrid and of course the gryphon. What passed in the fourth millennium for the playthings of a melancholy fantasy now reappear in the third millennium subjected to the rules of form and elevated to the cosmic level. Without doubt, this fascinating seal-roll could disclose the deepest secrets of the Elamite world picture if we only had the key to its mysterious code. But the Elamites would not have been Elamites if they had left written clues to this code.

Yet another unique achievement of third-millennium creative art in Elam are those perfect little jars of translucent alabaster which were found in a foundation-deposit in Susa. They often represent some kind of animal, frequently with humorous overtones. Such a one is the figure of a monkey, seated in a comically life-like position; or that of a stylized dove, which gazes in mute appeal at the world with its huge round eyes – and yet it is only a little scent-bottle.

Elam's art reached a point of glorious and unequalled maturity under the rule of King Untash-napirisha in the thirteenth century. The art of this period concerns us firstly because this was the acme of the skill of bronze-casting, and secondly because of the architectural plans and achievements that are in evidence at the site of the ziggurat founded by Untash-napirisha at Choga Zambil.

The so-called Luristan bronzes of the first millennium, which have in recent decades become world-famous, were based in my opinion on the accomplishments they had inherited from the highly developed bronzes of the second millennium and in particular of the thirteenth century. For example, I would agree with André Godard when he sees in the bronze axe which King Untash-napirisha dedicated to the ziggurat an earlier prototype of the Luristan bronzes. The bronze blade of the axe 'streams out' of the gaping jaws of a lion, and a gold or electron wild-boar cowers behind the handle-mounting. In subsequent years such decoration of battle-axes and cross-hatchets became more and more refined, culminating in the perfect and unexpected art-form of the Luristan bronzes. It is obvious from this that we must look for the original seat of all Elamite bronze art in Luristan, most likely in the north near modern Nehawand and Harsin.

Unquestionably the greatest example of Elamite bronze-casting is the statue of Untash-napirisha's wife, Napir-asu, already mentioned in Chapter VI, which was found in Susa (Plate 29). As ever, we are struck by the dignity and noble calm that radiates from this truly royal figure. Since the head is missing, our gaze is concentrated on the hands, crossed in prayer, and on their long and slender fingers. The statue was first modelled in wax, cast in two operations, and then carefully finished. The mere fact that the statue weighs nearly 1,800 kilograms indicates that the Elamite bronze-casters were not only artistically, but technically very advanced.

The greatest example of Elamite architecture, half-preserved even today, is the ziggurat at Choga Zambil (Dur-Untash). The ziggurats of Mesopotamia, even the biggest one at Ur, are in a far more serious state of dilapidation and disrepair than the Elamite 'tower of Babel'. It is also clear that where the site and form of their ziggurats were concerned, the independent Elamites deviated to a considerable degree from the Mesopotamians.

This ziggurat has already been described in part in Chapter III, where it led to certain conclusions about Elamite religion. Here I shall attempt to assess the building primarily as a technical and architectural achievement. At this point I shall refer to the foundation plans in Figure 39, which show it as it appeared in 1962, after Ghirshman had completed the excavations there.

Even at first glance over the site as a whole, it is clear that this was all conceived on the grand scale. The planner can have been no other than Untash-napirisha himself, but his surveillance does not seem to have led to any disruption of relations with his architects and labourers. A quick glance at Plates 8–13 will give us some idea of the vast labour force required for the completion of this huge building, which can bear comparison with any large-scale modern constructions. As a preliminary, millions of clay tiles and hundreds of thousands of baked bricks had to be prepared. The raw materials were to hand on the site itself, and water was provided by the river Diz, only one and a half kilometres away. But the provision of fuel needed for the large and beautiful paving and wall-tiles was tedious, time-consuming and expensive. Susiana, now almost devoid of trees (a state of affairs that the new dam on the Diz should correct) was equally short of wood in ancient times. And so wood for fuel had to be felled in the distant mountains of Luristan, carried by donkey and buffalo to the Diz, and then floated downstream.

For years, King Untash-napirisha was forced to mobilize a whole army of tens of thousands of tile-makers, brick-bakers, masons, navvies, handymen and donkey-drivers – and he also had to provide for them. He needed experts for the ingenious drainage and irrigation schemes of Dur-Untash; for the plans for the decoration of the walls in brightly painted mosaic; and for the countless sacred offerings in metal, marble, frit or glass. He needed a whole school of industrious scribes to letter the

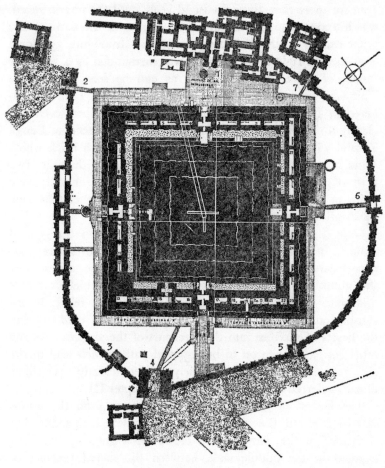

*Figure 39*

thousands of tiles, for all were written by hand: no stamps
were used. We must admit a certain admiration for the organi-
zational capacity of the Elamites.

And so to the details. The basic plan of the ziggurat in
Figure 39 is a square with a side of 105 metres. Thus each
side of the ziggurat measured at its base 200 Elamite ells; the
ell equalled $52\frac{1}{2}$ centimetres and remained almost unchanged in

Iran for more than three thousand years until the metric system was introduced in this century. The corners of the basic square point exactly to the four compass points. (In Figure 39, north is at the top right.) The ziggurat was surrounded by a wall, the inmost of three at Dur-Untash, as can be seen in Plate 9. This wall was provided with seven gates, which I have numbered in Figure 39 for easy reference. The number seven was clearly a significant one to the Elamites, and it recurs at Choga Zambil with the small sacrificial tables faced with brick which stand before the south-east steps of the ziggurat : there are two rows of seven tables each. Probably twice seven animals were slain on them during worship; the drainage runnel that took the overflow from the sacrificial blood is still visible.

Gate 3 near the southern corner deviates from the general pattern in that it alone is paved with hewn stones; the gaps between them are filled with bitumen. The stones show the unmistakable traces of two wheel-tracks, which indicates that gate 3 was used by carts. As it is also relatively inconspicuous, it seems likely that the gate was only used to bring the beasts of sacrifice into the forecourt of the ziggurat. All the other six gates open on to brick-paved paths which lead to the ziggurat; but they lead obliquely, never directly. We have already referred to this phenomenon in Chapter III.

The largest of the seven gates is number 4 on the south-eastern side, to the right of the 'cart-gate'; Ghirshman has christened it the 'king's gate'. However, a gateway has been exposed in the middle wall, between the sacred precinct of *Siyankuk* and the town of Dur-Untash, and according to the inscription it was called the 'great gateway' on the outside and the 'king's gateway' on the inside; and so we shall avoid confusion by referring to gate 4 as the 'king's gate of the ziggurat'.

As you can see in Figure 39, a square temple has been built in front of gates 2, 4 and 7. According to the inscriptions, the temple at gate 7 was dedicated to the god Humban. Next to it are sited two temples, both before gate 1 : on the far left, one to the goddess Ishnikarab and, between this and the temple of Humban, one to the great goddess Kiririsha. Similarly, there are still scattered remains of an outer temple at gate 6, but at gate 5 all traces of earlier construction have vanished. However, in spite of this, we can accept Ghirshman's suggestion that temples flanked the entrances to all the six gates through which worshippers entered the forecourt. Whoever wished to enter the inner sanctum had to do honour to the gods while still outside the wall of the ziggurat, and probably also make a small offering.

A knotty question is posed by the three circular buildings near the steps on all sides of the ziggurat except the south-east or 'king's side'. They are four metres in diameter and each possess four niches set into triple arches (Plate 12). An inscribed frieze runs round the base of each tower, from which we learn that these puzzling buildings were known in Elamite as *shunshu irpi* and were dedicated to the gods Humban and Inshushinak. This would solve everything, if we only knew what the words *shunshu irpi* meant. But since there is no such tower in the south-eastern forecourt, which appears to have been reserved for the king, we might identify these buildings as the bases that once held statues of the ruler, who would thus have been represented in stone on the three sides of the ziggurat where he was not present in the flesh.

Let us now turn to the sketch of Choga Zambil itself, where we once more feel firm ground beneath our feet.

As Ghirshman realized with his usual penetration, the ziggurat at Dur-Untash was not built in one operation but was put up in two distinct sections. This fact was suggested by a trial trench that was taken out from the north-west side to the middle of the ziggurat. This trench, excavated during the dig of 1960–61, is marked on the plan in Figure 39, and it established that in the first stage of construction only that portion of the site was put up which is reproduced in Figure 40, taken from a diagram by the architect P. Auberson.

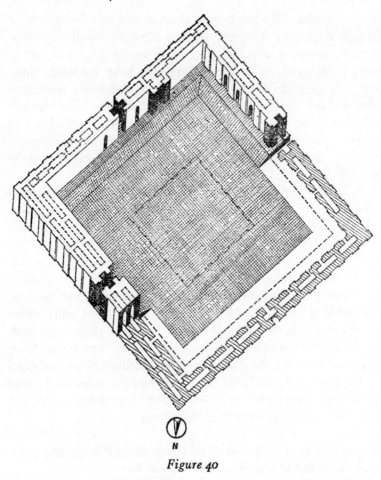

*Figure 40*

The first storey of the ziggurat, a square eight metres high, rose up around an inner courtyard almost a hundred metres square, which was carefully paved with baked tiles. This storey measured eight metres on three of its sides, but twelve on the fourth, the north-east. It may be referred to as the 'spectator side' of the ziggurat, as distinct from the south-east or 'king's side'. The square of the first storey contains twenty-eight rooms, many of which could only be reached by steps from above. Those that did have doors to the outside opened on to the inner court with the single exception of room 19 in Figure 39.

On the south-east side of the first storey, there are temples dedicated to the god Inshushinak on either side of the staircase. The temple opposite gate 4, which Ghirshman labels temple A, was apparently used for religious purposes only until the other storeys were added, when it was walled up. It was replaced by temple B opposite gave 5, with a door leading from room 19 into the south-east forecourt. Ghirshman correctly identified this temple as the 'low temple', which alternated with the high temple at the summit of the ziggurat for religious purposes. As early as 2250 we find corresponding arrangements at the Temple of Inshushinak at Susa; at this period King Kutik-Inshushinak dedicated daily sacrifices for its high temple and also for its low temple. But whereas in Mesopotamia the low temple was always outside, though close to, the ziggurat, Elamite principles clearly demanded that the low temple should form an integral part of the ziggurat.

Ghirshman has this to say about temple B :*

We must also mention another peculiarity of this small shrine : to the left of the ante-chamber it opened on to a room containing a bed made of clay tiles opposite a niche in the wall [he is clearly referring to room 18 in Figure 39]. Was this room perhaps intended as a resting-place for the deity, who would come down from his 'dwelling-place' at the top of the ziggurat? Or was it intended for some quite different purpose, that of a 'sacred marriage' (*hieros gamos*), as is indicated by the small terracotta models of a couple resting on a bed that are often unearthed in the Elamite levels at Susa?

In the course of the second stage of construction, storeys

* *Iranica Antiqua III*, Leiden, 1963, 13

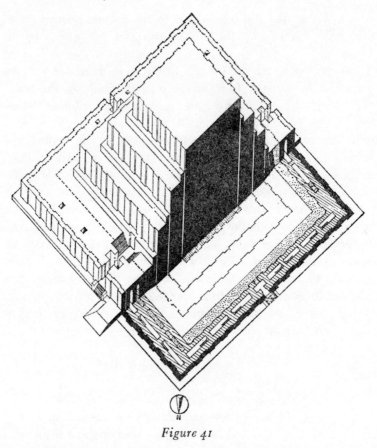

*Figure 41*

II, III and IV of the ziggurat were begun simultaneously. At this point we should consult the isometric diagram in Figure 41, drawn up by P. Auberson. It shows that the three top layers were built up from the floor of the courtyard, so that they rose up from the first storey like a nest of boxes. The pavement of the inmost court is thus only preserved underneath the central, fourth, stage.

It was on this fourth storey that the culmination of the whole vast edifice, the high temple to Inshushinak, was placed. Nothing now survives of this *kukunnum* (sometimes simply

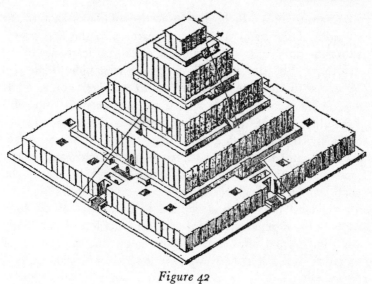

*Figure 42*

known as *huli*, or 'palace') except tiles that have fallen from
it, but in spite of this its measurements can be deduced with a
fair degree of accuracy. The floor of the fourth storey was a
square with a side of 35 metres, and so the high temple may
have measured 20 metres by 20. Its approximate height is also
discoverable; we have seen that the bottom storey of the ziggurat was 8 metres high, while the height was 11.55 at the
second and was probably the same for the third and fourth
storeys. This would mean that the base of the fourth storey lay
at a height of about 42.5 metres. But there are many indications
that the ziggurat was twice as wide as it was high, and if this
is so it would have reached a height of 100 Elamite ells, or
52.5 metres. We can thus attribute to the high temple an eleva-
tion of 10 metres, which would make it twice as wide as it was
high, just as the ziggurat itself was; all in all a most impressive
building, with a view into the distance as far as the ziggurat of
Susa.

The steps of the ziggurat are particularly interesting because
they are of quite different heights. As can be seen from Figures

39 and 42, there is a flight of steps in the middle of each of the four sides of the ziggurat. They all lead up to the first storey, and on the north-east and north-west sides they lead *only* to the first storey. But the steps on the south-west side (Plate 13) give access to the second as well as to the first storey, while those on the south-east side appear to have been the most impressive, as was after all only fitting on the 'king's side' (Figure 42). They begin opposite the 'king's gate of the ziggurat', between A and B, the two temples to Inshushinak, and mount straight up to the first, third and fourth storeys, by-passing the second, which was served by the south-west flight. Finally, a fifth flight on the fourth storey led to the portal of the high temple but – significantly – not as a continuation of the 'king's steps', but round the eastern corner, on the north-east or 'spectators' side'. And here we have a vivid impression of how irreverent it would have seemed to an Elamite to take a direct approach to the threshold of a shrine. It had to be made obliquely, or round the corner.

Finally, let me attempt to assemble all the individual details of the ziggurat site that we have described into a complete picture, and to call to mind all the relevant religious and historical events. Let us imagine a high festival of the Elamite calendar, for example the New Year celebrations on the first of Lanlube, at new moon of the autumnal equinox. King Untash-napirisha, his wife Napir-asu, his nephew Crown Prince Unpatar-napirisha, and other grandees, have arrived in their triumphal car from the royal precinct at the 'king's gate of the ziggurat' on the south-eastern side. After a short period of meditation in the temple to Humban before gate 4, the royal family entered through the same gate. There, priests poured water over the royal hands from a huge clay pitcher, whose remains have been discovered, as a ritual purification. Then the royal couple would take up their position, opposite the south-east steps, with their backs to the inner wall; their two brick rostra – a large one for the king, a smaller one on the right for his queen – still stand here.

Some time ago, the entire population of Dur-Untash had already started out in the direction of the north-east side of the ziggurat; those of the faithful who were privileged to participate had wended their way along every street, moving in long processions and according to an established order, with their hands crossed at the waist in prayer. The onlooker would notice in particular the three processions that formed up by the north-eastern entrance of the third wall and then wound its way with measured tread to converge on gates 5, 6 and 7. Inside the wall of the ziggurat, the elect took their stand on the tiled platforms which flanked the building on all four sides, but most people squeezed into the forecourt of the north-east 'spectator side'. The celebration of the service began to the accompaniment of music from voices, harps, lyres and flutes; the beasts of sacrifice were slain in the sight of the royal couple on the twice-seven sacrificial tables that stood in front of the south-east steps. Most likely, sacrifices also took place simultaneously at the other three sides of the ziggurat where the king was only present as a statue upon the round towers.

When the sacrifice was concluded, the elect made their way up the steps of the ziggurat; a throng of the lesser courtiers and the ordinary priests surged up to the first storey, using the stairs on the north-east and north-west. Those who were able found a place on the wide platform on the north-east, spectators' side, which was four metres wider than that on the other three sides of the ziggurat. The more important officials and dignatories reached the second storey from the south-west side, but then turned to the right round two corners of the ziggurat so that they too were on the north-east side.

Now the moment had come for Untash-napirisha to make a move. He strode between the two rows of altars to the foot of the south-east steps, poured a libation to the deity (the drainage runnel is still visible), and, followed by the senior priests and his more intimate courtiers, he embarked on a ceremonial ascent of the ziggurat. The lower members of his staff broke off from the procession on the third storey, and turned to the right round one corner to the north-east side. The ruler himself and his depleted suite continued the direct climb to the fourth storey, where he also turned off to the right round the eastern corner, and thus reached the foot of the steps that led up to the holiest shrine.

His suite halted at the north-east corner of the fourth storey; the tense and emotional crowds below gazed up at their ruler, who then mounted the steps to the high temple of Inshushinak, accompanied only by the high priest. At this moment, the shrine at the summit of the ziggurat dominated the whole of Susiana. Its mosaic walls, glazed gold, silver and ochre, and the huge horns cast in shining bronze which reared up from them, all glittered and sparkled in the autumn sun. The concourse of the faithful, clad in festal garb, and deep in silent prayer, watched breathlessly as King Untash-napirisha approached the high temple. The high priest opened the bronze portals for him, after anointing them with holy oil. Then the ruler entered the presence of the deity . . .

At this point I shall break off. We have no examples of Elam's later architectural achievements that are at all comparable with Choga Zambil. Some idea of post-classical Elamite art is conveyed in Plates 7, 14, 17, 18, 31 and 32. But at present those finds and monuments which have come to light do not justify a detailed description of the period; it is possible that the position may change if further digs are undertaken in Susiana, and in the mountains of Luristan and of the western Fars.

When Elam was incorporated into the Achaemenid Empire in 538, the Persians inherited its art and civilization. For some time before this, they had profited from an Elamite education; they had been countrymen and neighbours on their eastern border since about 695. Michael Rostovtzeff, in his *History of the Ancient World*,* even went so far as to claim that Cyrus the Great himself founded his culture and his ability to introduce political developments on the Elamite archetype. At any

* German translation by Hans Heinrich Schaeder, Leipzig, 1941, I, 131/2

rate, the culture that Iran inherited from Elam had a profound influence on its intellectual history, and its ramifications remain perceptible today.

An examination of these traces must await further and more detailed research. But students of the history and civilization of the ancient world will continue to be intrigued by the Elamite people, and the Kingdom of Elam will continue to withhold its secrets from generations of scholars.

# *Chronological Tables*

# *Genealogical Tables*

## House of the Eparti or 'grand regents'

(with the approximate dates of their reigns)

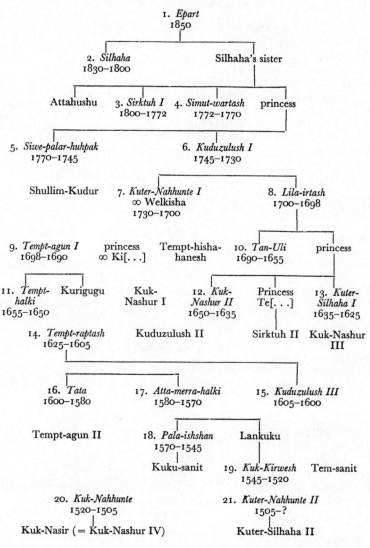

1. *Epart*
1850

2. *Silhaha*
1830–1800

Silhaha's sister

Attahushu

3. *Sirktuh I*
1800–1772

4. *Simut-wartash*
1772–1770

princess

5. *Siwe-palar-huhpak*
1770–1745

6. *Kuduzulush I*
1745–1730

Shullim-Kudur

7. *Kuter-Nahhunte I*
∞ Welkisha
1730–1700

8. *Lila-irtash*
1700–1698

9. *Tempt-agun I*
1698–1690

princess
∞ Ki[...]

Tempt-hisha-
hanesh

10. *Tan-Uli*
1690–1655

princess

11. *Tempt-*
*halki*
1655–1650

Kurigugu

Kuk-
Nashur I

12. *Kuk-*
*Nashur II*
1650–1635

Princess
Te[...]

13. *Kuter-*
*Silhaha I*
1635–1625

14. *Tempt-raptash*
1625–1605

Kuduzulush II

Sirktuh II

Kuk-Nashur
III

16. *Tata*
1600–1580

17. *Atta-merra-halki*
1580–1570

15. *Kuduzulush III*
1605–1600

Tempt-agun II

18. *Pala-ishshan*
1570–1545

Lankuku

Kuku-sanit

19. *Kuk-Kirwesh*
1545–1520

Tem-sanit

20. *Kuk-Nahhunte*
1520–1505

21. *Kuter-Nahhunte II*
1505–?

Kuk-Nasir (= Kuk-Nashur IV)

Kuter-Silhaha II

## House of the Igehalkids

(with the approximate dates of their reigns)

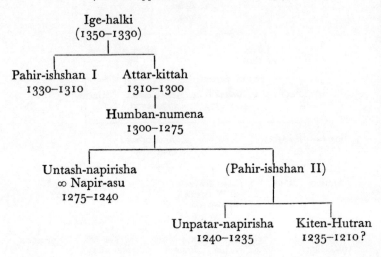

Ige-halki
(1350–1330)

Pahir-ishshan I
1330–1310

Attar-kittah
1310–1300

Humban-numena
1300–1275

Untash-napirisha
∞ Napir-asu
1275–1240

(Pahir-ishshan II)

Unpatar-napirisha
1240–1235

Kiten-Hutran
1235–1210?

## House of the Shutrukids

(with the approximate dates of their reigns)

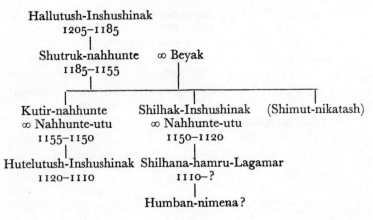

Hallutush-Inshushinak
1205–1185

Shutruk-nahhunte
1185–1155

∞ Beyak

Kutir-nahhunte
∞ Nahhunte-utu
1155–1150

Shilhak-Inshushinak
∞ Nahhunte-utu
1150–1120

(Shimut-nikatash)

Hutelutush-Inshushinak
1120–1110

Shilhana-hamru-Lagamar
1110–?

Humban-nimena?

*The Later Elamite Kings*

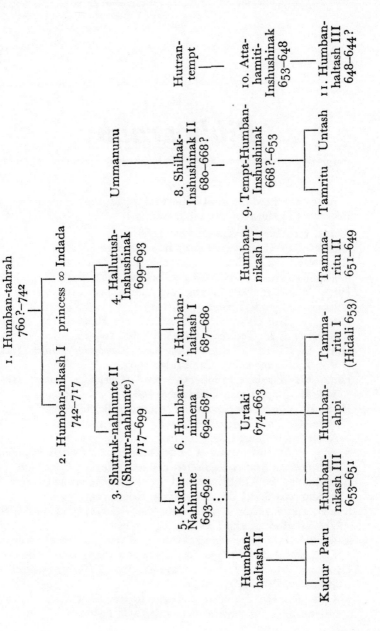

1. Humban-tahrah 760?–742
2. Humban-nikash I 742–717 — princess ∞ Indada
3. Shutruk-nahhunte II (Shutur-nahhunte) 717–699
4. Hallutush-Inshushinak 699–693
5. Kudur-Nahhunte 693–692
6. Humban-nimena 692–687
7. Humban-haltash I 687–680
8. Shilhak-Inshushinak II 680–668? — Ummanunu
9. Tempt-Humban-Inshushinak 668?–653
10. Atta-hamiti-Inshushinak 653–648
11. Humban-haltash III 648–644?
Hutran-tempt
Tamritu
Untash
Humban-haltash II
Urtaki 674–663
Humban-nikash II
Tamma-ritu II 651–649
Tamma-ritu I (Hidali 653)
Humban-ahpi
Humban-nikash III 653–651
Kudur Paru

185

# Bibliography

(I have only listed the most important works; they contain complete references to the relevant bibliography.)

AMIET, P., *Elam*, Anvers-sur-Oise 1966.

CAMERON, G. G. *History of Early Iran*. Chicago 1936.

GHIRSHMAN, R. 'L'Elam et les recherches à Dur-Untashi (Tchoga-Zanbil)'. In: *Iranica Antiqua* 3, Leiden 1963, 1–21.

HINZ, W. 'Zur Entzifferung der elamischen Strichschrift'. In: *Iranica Antiqua* 2, Leiden 1962, 1–17.

HINZ, W. 'Die elamischen Inschriften des Hanne'. In: *Volume in honour of S. H. Taqizadeh*, London 1962, 105–16.

HINZ, W. 'Persia c. 2400–1800 B.C.' (*Cambridge Ancient History*, Vol. I, chapter xxiii). Cambridge 1963.

HINZ, W. 'Persia c. 1800–1550 B.C.' (*Cambridge Ancient History*, Vol. II, chapter vii). Cambridge 1964.

HINZ, W. *Altiranische Funde und Forschungen*. Berlin 1969.

HÜSING, G. *Die einheimischen Quellen zur Geschichte Elams*. I. Teil: Altelamische Texte. Leipzig 1916.

KÖNIG, F. W. 'Mutterrecht und Thronfolge im alten Elam'. In: *Festschrift der Nationalbibliothek in Wien*. Wien 1926, 529–52.

KOSCHAKER, P. 'Göttliches und weltliches Recht nach den Urkunden aus Susa'. In: *Orientalia* 4, Rome 1935, 38–80.

LABAT, RENÉ. 'Elam c. 1600–1200 B.C.' (*Cambridge Ancient History*, Vol. II, chapter xxix). Cambridge 1963.

LABAT, RENÉ. 'Elam and Western Persia, c. 1200–1000 B.C.' (*Cambridge Ancient History*, Vol. II, chapter xxxii). Cambridge 1964.

LAMBERT, M. 'Littérature élamite'. In: *L'Histoire générale des littératures*, Paris 1961, 36–41.

MAYER, R. 'Die Bedeutung Elams in der Geschichte des alten Orients'. In: *Saeculum* 7, Freiburg 1956, 198–220.

*Mémoires de la délégation en Perse*, vols 1–3, Paris 1900–12; the title was subsequently changed several times, and the most recent (since 1968) is *Mémoires de la délégation archéologique en Iran*; vol. 42 appeared in Paris in 1970.

PARROT, A. *Sumer*. Munich 1960. (Includes many Elamite works of art.)

PORADA, EDITH. Ancient Iran. London 1965.

STEVE, M.-J. 'Textes élamites de Tchogha-Zanbil'. In: *Iranica Antiqua* 2, Leiden 1962, 22–76 and 3, 1963, 102–23.

VANDEN BERGHE, L. *Archéologie de l'Iran ancien*. Leiden 1959.

VANDEN BERGHE, L. 'Les reliefs élamites à Mālamīr'. In: *Iranica Antiqua* 3, Leiden 1963, 22–39.

WEISSBACH, F. H. *Die Keilinschriften der Achämeniden*. Leipzig 1911.

# Index

Abalgamash, King of Warahshi, 61
Achaemenes, dynasty, 138, 148
Adad, Babylonian god, 45
Adams, Robert M., 14
Akkad, 65–6; domination of Elam, 62
Akkadian script, replaces Elamite, 26–7
Al-Untash (Dur-Untash), founded, 103–6; *see also* Choga Zambil
Alexander the Great, in Iran, 5
Ali Kosh, 4
Amar-Su'ena, King of Sumeria, 70
Andreas, F. C., discovers Bushire barrow, 3
Anunitum, goddess, 51
Arian immigration, 126–7
Assarhaddon, King of Assyria, 139
Ashshur-dan, King of Assyria, defeated, 121
Assurbanipal, King of Assyria, 36, 45, 48, 54; asylum to Elamite princes, 141; captures Susa, 146–7; death, 147; decisive victory over Elam, 142–3; on Elamite attack on Mesopotamia, 85; on Tempt-Humban-Inshushinak, 142; ravages burial vaults, 56; restores goddess Nanaja, 86
Assyria, army occupies Elamite coastal towns, 136; army campaigns, 140–1; campaign by Elamites, 120–1; battle of Halule, 138–9; break with Elam, 141; campaign (646 B.C.) against Elam, 143–7; Sennacherib ascends

throne, 134; victory over Babylonia, 108–9
Atta-hamiti-Inshushinak, King, 144–5
Attahushu, Regent of Susa, innovations, 82
Attar-kittah, King, succession and title, 100
Auberson, P., 161–2
Awan dynasty, 67, 167
Ayahitek, stele plundered, 110–11

Babylonia, Assyrian victory, 108–9; battle of Halule, 138–9; capture of towns by Elamites, 112–13; defeats Elam forces, 124–5; inscriptions, 21–6, 105; occupied by Sennacherib, 134; Sargon ascends throne, 133; under Hammurabi, 83–4; victory over Elamite army, 108
Berghe, L. Vanden, 5, 41
Bork, F., on Elamite inscriptions, 21–2
Brice, W. C., 20
Burial customs, 55–7
Bushire, barrow discovered, 3; cult of Kiririsha, 33

Cameron, G. G., 28; on Naram-sin treaty, 63
Chicago University, 4
Choga Mish, excavations, 150
Choga Zambil, 3–4; 103–6; ziggurat, 43–5, 155–66
Cyrus the Great, ruler of all Elam, 148